Python Cookbook
100 Recipes for Programming

Table of Contents

25. Palindrome Checker

6. Collections (Lists, Dictionaries, Tuples, Sets):

26. Creating and Accessing Lists
27. List Operations (append(), insert(), remove(), sort(), reverse())
28. Dictionaries (key-value pairs, accessing, modifying)
29. Tuple Operations (packing, unpacking, indexing)
30. Set Operations (union, intersection, difference)

7. Boolean Operations & Control Flow:

31. Boolean Values (True, False) and Operators (and, or, not)
32. If, Elif, Else Statements
33. Comparison Operators (==, !=, <, >, <=, >=)
34. Nested Conditional Statements
35. Ternary Operator (x if condition else y)

8. Loops (For & While):

36. For Loops (iterating over sequences)
37. While Loops (condition-based iteration)
38. Break and Continue Statements
39. Nested Loops (pattern printing, matrix manipulation)
40. Infinite Loops (and how to avoid them)

9. Functions:

41. Defining and Calling Functions
42. Function Arguments (positional, keyword)
43. Return Values
44. Default Arguments and Variable-Length Arguments (*args, **kwargs)
45. Recursive Functions

10. File I/O:

46. Opening, Reading, and Writing Files
47. Working with Different File Modes (read, write, append)
48. File Paths and Directories
49. Reading and Writing CSV Files

Welcome to Python Cookbook: 100 Recipes for Programming Success

Are you ready to embark on a flavorful journey into the world of Python programming? Whether you're a novice taking your first steps or an experienced coder seeking to expand your repertoire, this cookbook is your passport to mastering the art of Python through hands-on practice.

Why a Cookbook?

In the culinary world, cookbooks offer a treasure trove of recipes, each a carefully crafted combination of ingredients and instructions that yield delicious results. Similarly, this Python cookbook presents you with 100 bite-sized, yet impactful, programs that serve as your building blocks for becoming a proficient Python chef.

Learn by Doing:

I believe that the best way to learn programming is by getting your hands dirty with code. That's why this book focuses on practical examples, guiding you through 100 carefully selected Python programs. Each program is a complete recipe, including:

- **Ingredients (Code):** The lines of Python code that make up the program.

- **Preparation (Explanation):** A clear and concise explanation of how the code works, breaking down the logic and concepts involved.

- **Final Dish (Output):** The result of running the code, so you can see the delicious outcome of your efforts.

From Appetizers to Main Courses:

Just like a well-balanced meal, this cookbook progresses through a variety of Python topics, starting with the fundamentals and gradually introducing more advanced concepts. You'll begin with simple "appetizer" programs that introduce you to variables, data types, and basic operations. As you gain confidence, you'll move on to more complex "main courses" covering topics like functions, file I/O, object-oriented programming, and even data analysis.

Who is this Cookbook For?

This cookbook is designed to be accessible to learners at all levels:

- **Beginners:** If you're new to Python, the early chapters will gently introduce you to the core concepts and syntax.

- **Intermediate Learners:** You'll find plenty of recipes to deepen your understanding and expand your skills.

- **Experienced Programmers:** Even seasoned Pythonistas can discover new techniques and best practices.

How to Use this Cookbook:

1. **Don't just read – code!** Type out each program yourself, experiment with modifications, and see how the output changes.

2. **Embrace the errors:** Mistakes are a natural part of learning. Don't be discouraged; use them as opportunities to troubleshoot and grow.

3. **Get creative:** Once you've mastered the basics, try adapting the recipes to solve your own unique problems or create your own programs.

Ready to Cook Up Some Python Magic?

Turn the page and let's get started! With 100 recipes at your fingertips, you'll be well on your way to becoming a Python pro. Let's start!

Copyright

Disclaimer:

The information contained in this book is for educational purposes only. The author and publisher assume no responsibility for errors or omissions, or for damages resulting from the use of the information in this book. The reader is responsible for verifying the accuracy and relevance of the information presented herein.

Trademark Acknowledgements:

Python is a registered trademark of the Python Software Foundation. All other trademarks and registered trademarks mentioned in this book are the property of their respective owners.

Contact Information:

For permissions or inquiries, please contact:

Ashish Prasad

ashishprasad133@gmail.com

1. Hello World & Basics:

Recipe 1: Hello, World!

Ingredients (Code):

```python
# Python
print("Hello, World!")
```

Preparation (Explanation):

This one-liner is the simplest Python program you can write. Let's break it down:

- **print():** This is a built-in Python function. Its job is to display information on your screen.

- **"Hello, World!":** This is the text you want to display. It's enclosed in quotation marks to indicate that it's a string of characters (a sequence of letters, numbers, or symbols).

When you run this code, the print() function takes the string "Hello, World!" and sends it to your console (the text output area of your development environment), where it appears as a greeting.

Final Dish (Output):

```
Hello, World!
```

Why is this important?

- **Milestone:** The "Hello, World!" program is a tradition in programming. It's often the first program you write when learning a new language, marking your entry into the world of coding.

- **Testing:** It's a quick way to check if your Python environment is set up correctly. If you see the output, you know your Python interpreter is working as expected.

- **Building Block:** While simple, this program introduces you to the fundamental concept of outputting information using functions, a key skill for any Python programmer.

Recipe 2: Basic Input and Output (Taking Input, Printing to Console)

Ingredients (Code):

```python
# Python
name = input("What's your name? ")
print(f"Hello, {name}! Welcome to the world of Python.")
```

Preparation (Explanation):

This program interacts with the user and provides a personalized greeting. Here's the breakdown:

1. **input("What's your name? "):**

   - The input() function prompts the user to enter their name. The text inside the parentheses is displayed as a message in the console.

   - The user's input is stored in the name variable as a string (a sequence of characters).

2. **print(f"Hello, {name}! Welcome to the world of Python."):**

   - The print() function displays the message in the console.

   - The f before the opening quotation mark indicates an f-string, a convenient way to embed variables directly into strings.

   - The {name} placeholder is replaced with the actual value of the name variable during the print operation.

Final Dish (Output):

```
What's your name? Alice
Hello, Alice! Welcome to the world of Python.
```

(The output will vary depending on the name entered by the user.)

Why is this important?

- **User Interaction:** This program demonstrates how to make your Python scripts interactive by accepting input from the user. This opens up possibilities for creating programs that respond to user actions and choices.

- **Personalized Output:** By combining user input with output, you can tailor the program's response, making it more engaging and relevant to the user.

- **String Formatting (f-strings):** This recipe introduces f-strings, a powerful feature in modern Python for creating clean and readable string output.

Recipe 3: Variable Assignment and Data Types (int, float, str)

Ingredients (Code):

```python
# Python
# Integer
age = 30

# Floating-point number
price = 19.99

# String
message = "Python is fun!"

# Print values and types
print(f"Age: {age}, Type: {type(age)}")
print(f"Price: {price}, Type: {type(price)}")
print(f"Message: {message}, Type: {type(message)}")
```

Preparation (Explanation):

1. Variable Assignment:

- **age = 30:** This line creates a variable named age and assigns it the integer value 30. Integers represent whole numbers.

- **price = 19.99:** This line creates a variable named price and assigns it the floating-point value 19.99. Floating-point numbers represent numbers with decimals.

- **message = "Python is fun!":** This line creates a variable named message and assigns it the string value "Python is fun!". Strings represent sequences of characters enclosed in quotation marks.

2. Printing Values and Types:

- **print(f"Age: {age}, Type: {type(age)}"):** This line prints the value of the age variable, followed by its data type, which is obtained using the type() function.

- The same pattern is repeated for the price and message variables.

Final Dish (Output):

```
Age: 30, Type: <class 'int'>
Price: 19.99, Type: <class 'float'>
Message: Python is fun!, Type: <class 'str'>
```

Why is this important?

- **Variables:** Variables are the fundamental building blocks of Python programs. They allow you to store and manipulate data, making your code dynamic and reusable.

- **Data Types:** Understanding data types is crucial because Python treats different types of data differently.

  - Integers are used for counting and arithmetic operations.

  - Floating-point numbers are essential for precise calculations involving decimals.

  - Strings are used to represent text and are often used for user input and output.

- **type() Function:** The type() function is a helpful tool to determine the data type of a variable, which can be essential for debugging and understanding how your code works.

- **F-Strings:** This recipe uses f-strings again, which provide an efficient and readable way to incorporate variable values into string outputs.

Recipe 4: Simple Arithmetic Operations (+, -, , /, //, %)

Ingredients (Code):

```python
# Python
num1 = 10
num2 = 3

# Addition
sum_result = num1 + num2
print(f"Sum: {num1} + {num2} = {sum_result}")

# Subtraction
difference_result = num1 - num2
print(f"Difference: {num1} - {num2} =
{difference_result}")

# Multiplication
product_result = num1 * num2
print(f"Product: {num1} * {num2} = {product_result}")

# Division
division_result = num1 / num2
print(f"Division: {num1} / {num2} = {division_result}")

# Floor Division
floor_division_result = num1 // num2
print(f"Floor Division: {num1} // {num2} =
{floor_division_result}")

# Modulus (Remainder)
modulus_result = num1 % num2
print(f"Modulus: {num1} % {num2} = {modulus_result}")
```

Preparation (Explanation):

1. **Variable Assignment:**

   - **num1 = 10:** Assigns the integer value 10 to the variable num1.

   - **num2 = 3:** Assigns the integer value 3 to the variable num2.

2. **Arithmetic Operations:**

- **sum_result = num1 + num2:** Calculates the sum of num1 and num2 and stores it in the variable sum_result.

- **difference_result = num1 - num2:** Calculates the difference between num1 and num2 and stores it in the variable difference_result.

- **product_result = num1 * num2:** Calculates the product of num1 and num2 and stores it in the variable product_result.

- **division_result = num1 / num2:** Calculates the division of num1 by num2, resulting in a floating-point number, and stores it in the variable division_result.

- **floor_division_result = num1 // num2:** Calculates the floor division of num1 by num2, resulting in the integer quotient (rounded down), and stores it in the variable floor_division_result.

- **modulus_result = num1 % num2:** Calculates the remainder when num1 is divided by num2 and stores it in the variable modulus_result.

3. **Printing Results:**

- The print() function is used to display the results of each operation using f-strings for clear formatting.

Final Dish (Output):

```
Sum: 10 + 3 = 13
Difference: 10 - 3 = 7
Product: 10 * 3 = 30
Division: 10 / 3 = 3.3333333333333335
Floor Division: 10 // 3 = 3
Modulus: 10 % 3 = 1
```

Why is this important?

- **Basic Math:** Arithmetic operations are the foundation of many computations in programming.

- **Operator Precedence:** Python follows the standard mathematical order of operations (PEMDAS/BODMAS).

- **Integer vs. Floating-Point Division:** / always results in a float, while // gives you an integer.

- **Modulus:** The modulus operator (%) is useful for tasks like checking if a number is even or odd, or for working with cyclic patterns.

Recipe 5: Type Conversion (str to int, float to str, etc.)

Ingredients (Code):

```python
# Python
# String to integer
age_str = "30"
age_int = int(age_str)
print(f"Age (str): {age_str}, Age (int): {age_int},
Type: {type(age_int)}")

# String to float
price_str = "19.99"
price_float = float(price_str)
print(f"Price (str): {price_str}, Price (float):
{price_float}, Type: {type(price_float)}")

# Integer to string
number = 42
number_str = str(number)
print(f"Number (int): {number}, Number (str):
{number_str}, Type: {type(number_str)}")

# Float to string
pi = 3.14159
pi_str = str(pi)
print(f"Pi (float): {pi}, Pi (str): {pi_str}, Type:
{type(pi_str)}")

# Boolean to string
is_valid = True
is_valid_str = str(is_valid)
print(f"Valid (bool): {is_valid}, Valid (str):
{is_valid_str}, Type: {type(is_valid_str)}")
```

Preparation (Explanation):

1. **String to Integer (int()):**

   - **age_str = "30":** Creates a string variable age_str containing the characters "30".

   - **age_int = int(age_str):** Converts the string age_str into an integer using the int() function. This is possible because the string represents a valid whole number. The result is stored in age_int.

2. **String to Float (float()):**

- **price_str = "19.99":** Creates a string variable price_str containing the characters "19.99".

- **price_float = float(price_str):** Converts the string price_str into a floating-point number using the float() function. This works because the string represents a valid decimal number.

3. **Integer/Float to String (str()):**

- **number = 42:** Creates an integer variable number.

- **number_str = str(number):** Converts the integer number into a string.

- The same process is applied to the float pi.

4. **Boolean to String (str()):**

- **is_valid = True:** Creates a Boolean variable is_valid.

- **is_valid_str = str(is_valid):** Converts the Boolean is_valid to the string "True."

Final Dish (Output):

```
Age (str): 30, Age (int): 30, Type: <class 'int'>
Price (str): 19.99, Price (float): 19.99, Type: <class
'float'>
Number (int): 42, Number (str): 42, Type: <class 'str'>
Pi (float): 3.14159, Pi (str): 3.14159, Type: <class
'str'>
Valid (bool): True, Valid (str): True, Type: <class
'str'>
```

Why is this important?

- **Data Type Flexibility:** Type conversion allows you to work with data in different formats, which is essential for tasks like handling user input (often received as strings), performing calculations, and formatting output.

- **Input Handling:** User input from input() is always a string. You'll often need to convert this to numbers for calculations.

- **Output Formatting:** Converting numbers and Booleans to strings allows you to incorporate them into formatted messages or display them in a user-friendly way.

2. Numbers & Operations:

Recipe 6: Working with Numbers (Complex Numbers, Math Functions)

Ingredients (Code):

```python
# Python
import cmath  # Import the complex math module
import math   # Import the standard math module

# Complex numbers
z1 = 2 + 3j
z2 = 4 - 1j

# Basic operations on complex numbers
sum_result = z1 + z2
difference_result = z1 - z2
product_result = z1 * z2
division_result = z1 / z2

print(f"Complex Number Sum: {sum_result}")
print(f"Complex Number Difference: {difference_result}")
print(f"Complex Number Product: {product_result}")
print(f"Complex Number Division: {division_result}")

# Common math functions
x = 16
y = 2.5

# Square root
sqrt_result = math.sqrt(x)

# Power
power_result = math.pow(x, y)

# Absolute value
abs_result = abs(-5)

# Trigonometric functions (radians)
sin_result = math.sin(math.pi / 2)  # Sine of pi/2
cos_result = math.cos(0)  # Cosine of 0
tan_result = math.tan(math.pi / 4)  # Tangent of pi/4

print(f"Square root of {x}: {sqrt_result}")
print(f"{x} raised to the power {y}: {power_result}")
print(f"Absolute value of -5: {abs_result}")
print(f"Sine of pi/2: {sin_result}")
print(f"Cosine of 0: {cos_result}")
print(f"Tangent of pi/4: {tan_result}")
```

Preparation (Explanation):

1. Importing Modules:

- **import cmath:** Imports the cmath module, which provides functions for working with complex numbers.

- **import math:** Imports the standard math module, which contains a wide range of mathematical functions for real numbers.

2. Complex Numbers:

- **z1 = 2 + 3j:** Creates a complex number with real part 2 and imaginary part 3.

- **z2 = 4 - 1j:** Creates another complex number.

- The code demonstrates basic arithmetic operations on complex numbers (+, -, *, /).

3. Math Functions:

- **math.sqrt(x):** Calculates the square root of x.

- **math.pow(x, y):** Calculates x raised to the power y.

- **abs(-5):** Calculates the absolute value of -5 (distance from zero).

- math.sin(), math.cos(), math.tan(): Calculate trigonometric functions (sine, cosine, tangent) using radian inputs.

Final Dish (Output):

```
Complex Number Sum: (6 + 2j)
Complex Number Difference: (-2 + 4j)
Complex Number Product: (11 + 10j)
Complex Number Division: (0.2 + 0.8j)
```

```
Square root of 16: 4.0
16 raised to the power 2.5: 1024.0
Absolute value of -5: 5
Sine of pi/2: 1.0
Cosine of 0: 1.0
Tangent of pi/4: 0.9999999999999999
```

Why is this important?

- **Complex Numbers:** Complex numbers are used in various fields like physics, engineering, and signal processing. Python's cmath module provides tools to work with them.

- **Math Functions:** The math module offers a vast collection of functions for mathematical operations, making complex calculations easier. Understanding these functions is crucial for solving problems in science, engineering, and data analysis.

Recipe 7: Number Formatting (Rounding, Precision)

Ingredients (Code):

```python
# Python
import math

pi = math.pi  # Get the value of pi
e = math.e    # Get Euler's number

# Rounding
rounded_pi = round(pi, 2)    # Round pi to 2 decimal
places
rounded_e = round(e)         # Round e to the nearest
integer

print(f"Pi (original): {pi}")
print(f"Pi (rounded to 2 decimal places): {rounded_pi}")
print(f"Euler's number (original): {e}")
print(f"Euler's number (rounded to nearest integer):
{rounded_e}")

# String formatting for precision
formatted_pi = "{:.4f}".format(pi)  # Format pi to 4
decimal places
formatted_e = "{:.3f}".format(e)    # Format e to 3
decimal places

print(f"Pi (formatted to 4 decimal places):
{formatted_pi}")
print(f"Euler's number (formatted to 3 decimal places):
{formatted_e}")

# Percentage formatting
percentage = 0.75
formatted_percentage = "{:.1%}".format(percentage)   #
Format as percentage with 1 decimal

print(f"Percentage: {formatted_percentage}")
```

Preparation (Explanation):

1. **Import the math module:** This line imports the math module, which contains mathematical constants and functions like pi (π) and e.

2. **Rounding with round():**

- **round(pi, 2):** Rounds the value of pi to 2 decimal places.

- **round(e):** Rounds e to the nearest integer (default behavior when no second argument is given).

3. **String Formatting with format():**

   - **"{:.4f}".format(pi):** Formats pi as a floating-point number with 4 decimal places. The :.4f inside the curly braces specifies the format.

   - **"{:.3f}".format(e):** Formats e with 3 decimal places.

4. **Percentage Formatting:**

   - **"{:.1%}".format(percentage):** Formats percent age (0.75) as a percentage ("75.0%") with 1 decimal place.

Final Dish (Output):

```
Pi (original): 3.141592653589793
Pi (rounded to 2 decimal places): 3.14
Euler's number (original): 2.718281828459045
Euler's number (rounded to nearest integer): 3
Pi (formatted to 4 decimal places): 3.1416
Euler's number (formatted to 3 decimal places): 2.718
Percentage: 75.0%
```

Why is this important?

- **Precision Control:** In many applications, you'll need to control the precision of numerical values, either for display or for calculations.

- **Rounding:** Rounding is essential when you need approximate values or want to avoid overly precise results.

- **Formatting for Readability:** Formatting numbers with the correct number of decimal places or as percentages makes your output more clear and understandable to users.

- **format() Method:** The format() method is a versatile way to format numbers (and other data types) in strings, allowing for fine-grained control over how they appear.

Recipe 8: Bitwise Operations (&, |, ^, ~, <<, >>)

Ingredients (Code):

```python
# Python
a = 5        # Binary: 0101
b = 9        # Binary: 1001

# Bitwise AND (&)
result_and = a & b
print(f"{a} & {b} = {result_and}   (Binary:
{result_and:04b})")

# Bitwise OR (|)
result_or = a | b
print(f"{a} | {b} = {result_or}   (Binary:
{result_or:04b})")

# Bitwise XOR (^)
result_xor = a ^ b
print(f"{a} ^ {b} = {result_xor}   (Binary:
{result_xor:04b})")

# Bitwise NOT (~)
result_not_a = ~a
print(f"~{a} = {result_not_a}   (Binary:
{result_not_a:04b})")

# Left Shift (<<)
result_left_shift = a << 2
print(f"{a} << 2 = {result_left_shift}   (Binary:
{result_left_shift:04b})")

# Right Shift (>>)
result_right_shift = b >> 2
print(f"{b} >> 2 = {result_right_shift}   (Binary:
{result_right_shift:04b})")
```

Preparation (Explanation):

1. **Binary Representation:** Numbers in Python are internally stored as binary digits (0 and 1). The code assigns decimal values 5 (binary 0101) and 9 (binary 1001) to variables a and b, respectively.

2. **Bitwise Operators:**

- **& (AND):** Compares corresponding bits of two numbers. The result is 1 only if both bits are 1.

- **| (OR):** Compares corresponding bits of two numbers. The result is 1 if either bit is 1.

- **^ (XOR):** Compares corresponding bits of two numbers. The result is 1 only if the bits are different.

- **~ (NOT):** Inverts all bits of a number (0s become 1s, and vice versa).

- **<< (Left Shift):** Shifts the bits of a number to the left by the specified amount, filling in zeros on the right.

- **>> (Right Shift):** Shifts the bits of a number to the right by the specified amount, filling in the leftmost bit with a copy of itself (sign-extension for negative numbers).

3. **Formatting:** The :04b format specifier in the print statements ensures that the binary results are displayed with leading zeros, making them easier to read.

Final Dish (Output):

```
5 & 9 = 1    (Binary: 0001)
5 | 9 = 13   (Binary: 1101)
5 ^ 9 = 12   (Binary: 1100)
~5 = -6   (Binary: 11010)
5 << 2 = 20   (Binary: 10100)
9 >> 2 = 2    (Binary: 0010)
```

Why is this important?

- **Low-Level Operations:** Bitwise operators work directly on the binary representation of numbers, providing fine-grained control over individual bits. This is essential for tasks like setting flags, manipulating permissions, and working with hardware.

- **Optimization:** Bitwise operations are often faster than arithmetic operations, making them useful for optimizing code in performance-critical situations.

- **Applications:** Bitwise operators are used in cryptography, data compression, networking protocols, and many other areas of computer science.

Recipe 9: Random Number Generation

Ingredients (Code):

```python
# Python
import random

# Generate a random integer between 1 and 10 (inclusive)
random_integer = random.randint(1, 10)
print(f"Random Integer: {random_integer}")

# Generate a random floating-point number between 0 and
1 (exclusive)
random_float = random.random()
print(f"Random Float: {random_float}")

# Choose a random element from a list
fruits = ["apple", "banana", "orange", "grape"]
random_fruit = random.choice(fruits)
print(f"Random Fruit: {random_fruit}")

# Shuffle a list in-place
numbers = [1, 2, 3, 4, 5]
random.shuffle(numbers)
print(f"Shuffled Numbers: {numbers}")

# Sample multiple random items from a list without
replacement
lottery_numbers = random.sample(range(1, 50), 6)   #
Choose 6 numbers from 1 to 49
print(f"Lottery Numbers: {lottery_numbers}")
```

Preparation (Explanation):

1. **Import the random module:** This line imports the random module, which provides functions for generating random numbers and making random choices.

2. **Random Integer (random.randint(a, b)):**

   - Generates a random integer within the specified range (inclusive).

   - In our example, it will be a number between 1 and 10.

3. **Random Float (random.random()):**

- Generates a random floating-point number between 0 and 1 (the upper limit 1 is excluded).

4. **Random Choice (random.choice(sequence)):**

- Selects a random element from the given sequence (list, tuple, string, etc.).

- In our example, it chooses a random fruit from the fruits list.

5. **Shuffle (random.shuffle(sequence)):**

- Randomly reorders the elements of the given sequence in place.

- In our example, it shuffles the numbers list.

6. **Sample (random.sample(population, k)):**

- Chooses k unique random elements from the population sequence without replacement (no duplicates).

- In our example, it simulates picking 6 lottery numbers from 1 to 49.

Final Dish (Output):

```
Random Integer: 7
Random Float: 0.23908712486320853
Random Fruit: orange
Shuffled Numbers: [3, 5, 4, 2, 1]
Lottery Numbers: [13, 47, 21, 40, 8, 35]
```

(The output will vary each time you run the code due to the random nature of the functions.)

Why is this important?

- **Simulations:** Random numbers are essential for simulations, games, and modeling real-world scenarios with an element of chance.

- **Data Science:** Random sampling and shuffling are used in data analysis and machine learning for tasks like splitting datasets, cross-validation, and generating random test cases.

- **Security:** Random numbers are used in cryptography for generating keys and nonces.

- **Decision-Making:** Random choices can be used in algorithms that need to make unpredictable decisions.

Recipe 10: Prime Number Checker

Ingredients (Code):

```python
# Python
def is_prime(num):
  """Checks if a number is prime."""
  if num <= 1:   # 1 and numbers less than 1 are not
prime
    return False
  for i in range(2, int(num**0.5) + 1): # Check for
divisibility from 2 to sqrt(num)
    if num % i == 0:
      return False
  return True

# Example usage
number = 17
if is_prime(number):
  print(f"{number} is a prime number.")
else:
  print(f"{number} is not a prime number.")
```

Preparation (Explanation):

1. **Function Definition:**

   - **def is_prime(num):** Defines a function named is_prime that takes one argument, num, the number to be checked.

2. **Base Cases:**

   - **if num <= 1:** Checks if the number is less than or equal to 1. If so, it's not a prime number by definition, so the function immediately returns False.

3. **Check for Divisibility:**

   o **for i in range(2, int(num**0.5) + 1)::** This loop iterates through numbers from 2 up to the square root of num (inclusive). Why the square root? If a number has a divisor greater than its square root, it must also have a divisor smaller than its square root.

- o **if num % i == o:** Checks if num is divisible by the current value of i. If so, num is not prime, and the function returns False.

4. **Prime Confirmation:**

- **return True:** If the loop completes without finding a divisor, the number is prime, and the function returns True.

5. **Example Usage:**

- **number = 17:** Assigns the value 17 to the variable number.

- **is_prime(number):** Calls the is_prime function to check if number is prime.

- The if...else statement prints the appropriate message based on the function's return value.

Final Dish (Output):

```
17 is a prime number.
```

Why is this important?

- **Prime Numbers:** Prime numbers are fundamental in number theory and have applications in cryptography, computer science, and other fields.

- **Efficient Algorithm:** This implementation checks for divisibility only up to the square root of the number, making it more efficient than checking all the way up to num - 1.

- **Modular Functions:** The use of a function demonstrates modularity in programming, making the code reusable for checking different numbers.

Additional Notes:

- You can add a check for whether the input is an integer. You might include code to ask the user to try again if a non-integer was provided, using another input() function to get a new entry.

3. Strings Basics:

Recipe 11: String Concatenation and Replication

Ingredients (Code):

```python
# Python
greeting = "Hello"
name = "Alice"

# Concatenation using + operator
message1 = greeting + ", " + name + "!"
print(message1)

# Concatenation using join() method
words = ["Hello", "there", name]
message2 = " ".join(words)
print(message2)

# String replication using * operator
separator = "-" * 10
print(separator)
```

Preparation (Explanation):

1. **String Concatenation:**

   - **+ Operator:** The plus (+) operator is the most straightforward way to join strings together.

     - In the example, greeting + ", " + name + "!" combines the strings "Hello", ", ", "Alice", and "!" to create the message "Hello, Alice!".

   - **join() Method:** The join() method provides a more flexible way to concatenate strings, especially when dealing with lists or other sequences of strings.

     - It takes a sequence of strings as input and inserts the specified delimiter (in this case, a space " ") between each element.

2. **String Replication:**

- *** Operator:** The asterisk (*) operator is used to repeat a string a specified number of times.

    - In the example, "-" * 10 creates a string of 10 hyphens ("----------"), which can be used as a separator.

Final Dish (Output):

```
Hello, Alice!
Hello there Alice
```
___

Why is this important?

- **Building Strings:** String concatenation is essential for dynamically constructing messages, combining user input with fixed text, and creating formatted output.

- **Flexibility:** Python offers multiple ways to concatenate strings, giving you flexibility to choose the most appropriate method based on your specific requirements.

- **Visual Presentation:** String replication is useful for creating visual elements in text-based interfaces, such as separators, borders, or repeating patterns.

Additional Notes:

- **F-strings:** While the examples above demonstrate concatenation using + and join(), Python also offers f-strings (introduced in Python 3.6) as a more concise and readable way to embed variables within strings.

- **Performance:** When concatenating a large number of strings, using the join() method is generally more efficient than repeated use of the + operator.

Recipe 12: Escape Characters in Strings

Ingredients (Code):

```python
# Python
# Newline
print("This is the first line.\nThis is the second
line.")

# Tab
print("Name:\tAlice")

# Backslash
print("This string contains a backslash: \\")

# Single quote inside a single-quoted string
print('She said, "Hello!"')

# Double quote inside a double-quoted string
print("He said, \"Goodbye!\"")
```

Preparation (Explanation):

Escape characters are special characters preceded by a backslash (\) that have a specific meaning within a string. They allow you to insert characters that are otherwise difficult or impossible to include directly. Here's how each escape character is used in this recipe:

- **\n (Newline):** Inserts a line break, moving the following text to the next line.

- **\t (Tab):** Inserts a tab character, typically used for aligning text.

- **\\ (Backslash):** Represents a single backslash character itself. Since a backslash is used to signal escape sequences, you need two of them to include a literal backslash in a string.

- **\' or \" (Quotes):** Used to insert a single or double quote within a string that is already delimited by the same type of quote. For example, 'She said, "Hello!"' allows

41

you to include double quotes within a single-quoted string.

Final Dish (Output):

```
This is the first line.
This is the second line.
Name:    Alice
This string contains a backslash: \
She said, "Hello!"
He said, "Goodbye!"
```

Why is this important?

- **Formatting Text:** Escape characters provide a way to control the layout and appearance of your string output, making it more readable and visually appealing.

- **Representing Special Characters:** They enable you to include characters that cannot be typed directly, such as newlines and tabs.

- **Including Quotes:** Escape characters are essential for including quotes within strings, which is often necessary for displaying dialogue or other types of text that contain quotation marks.

Recipe 13: String Length and Membership (in, not in)

Ingredients (Code):

```python
# Python
sentence = "Python is a powerful programming language."

# String Length
length = len(sentence)
print(f"Length of the sentence: {length}")

# Membership (in)
substring = "powerful"
if substring in sentence:
    print(f"'{substring}' is found in the sentence.")
else:
    print(f"'{substring}' is not found in the
sentence.")

# Membership (not in)
substring = "Java"
if substring not in sentence:
    print(f"'{substring}' is not found in the
sentence.")
else:
    print(f"'{substring}' is found in the sentence.")
```

Preparation (Explanation):

1. **String Length (len()):**

    - The len() function is used to determine the number of characters in a string.

    - len(sentence) calculates the length of the string stored in the sentence variable.

2. **Membership (in):**

    - The in operator checks if a substring exists within a larger string. It returns True if the substring is found and False otherwise.

    - The code checks if "powerful" is present within the sentence.

3. **Membership (**not in**):**

- The not in operator is the opposite of in. It returns True if the substring is *not* found and False if it is found.

- The code checks if "Java" is not present within the sentence.

Final Dish (Output):

```
Length of the sentence: 40
'powerful' is found in the sentence.
'Java' is not found in the sentence.
```

Why is this important?

- **String Analysis:** Determining the length of a string is crucial for tasks like validation (ensuring usernames or passwords meet length requirements) and formatting (truncating long text).

- **Substring Search:** The in and not in operators are powerful tools for searching text. They can be used for filtering data, verifying input, or simply checking if a certain word or phrase appears in a document.

Additional Notes:

- **Case Sensitivity:** The in and not in operators are case-sensitive. If you want case-insensitive search, you can convert both the string and the substring to lowercase (or uppercase) before using these operators.

- **Performance Considerations:** If you need to perform a large number of substring searches in a very long string, consider using more advanced search algorithms like the Knuth-Morris-Pratt (KMP) algorithm or the Boyer-Moore algorithm for better performance.

Recipe 14: String Methods (lower(), upper(), split(), replace())

Ingredients (Code):

```python
# Python
text = "This is a Sample String with some MiXeD CaSe."

# lower() method
lowercase_text = text.lower()
print(f"Lowercase: {lowercase_text}")

# upper() method
uppercase_text = text.upper()
print(f"Uppercase: {uppercase_text}")

# split() method
words = text.split()
print(f"Words: {words}")

# replace() method
replaced_text = text.replace("MiXeD CaSe", "consistent style")
print(f"Replaced: {replaced_text}")
```

Preparation (Explanation):

1. **lower() Method:**

   - Converts all characters in the string to lowercase.

   - Useful for case-insensitive comparisons or standardizing text format.

2. **upper() Method:**

   - Converts all characters in the string to uppercase.

   - Can be used for emphasis or ensuring consistent capitalization.

3. **split() Method:**

   - Splits the string into a list of words based on whitespace (spaces, tabs, newlines) by default.

- You can specify a different delimiter character if needed.

- Useful for breaking down sentences or analyzing text content.

4. **replace(old, new) Method:**

- Replaces all occurrences of the old substring with the new substring.

- Allows you to modify specific parts of a string without changing the rest.

Final Dish (Output):

```
Lowercase: this is a sample string with some mixed case.
Uppercase: THIS IS A SAMPLE STRING WITH SOME MIXED CASE.
Words: ['This', 'is', 'a', 'Sample', 'String', 'with',
'some', 'MiXeD', 'CaSe.']
Replaced: This is a Sample String with some consistent
style.
```

Why is this important?

- **Text Manipulation:** String methods are fundamental tools for working with text data in Python. They enable you to clean, transform, and analyze text for various purposes.

- **Case Conversion:** lower() and upper() are often used to normalize text for comparisons or to conform to specific formatting styles.

- **Tokenization:** split() is a common technique for breaking down text into smaller units (words, phrases) for further processing, such as in natural language processing (NLP) tasks.

- **String Editing:** replace() allows you to make targeted changes to strings, which is useful for correcting errors, updating information, or customizing output.

Recipe 15: String Formatting (f-strings, %-formatting)

Ingredients (Code):

```python
# Python
name = "Alice"
age = 30
pi = 3.14159

# F-string formatting (Python 3.6+)
message_fstring = f"Hello, {name}! You are {age} years
old."
pi_fstring = f"The value of pi is approximately
{pi:.2f}"  # 2 decimal places

# %-formatting (older style)
message_percent = "Hello, %s! You are %d years old." %
(name, age)
pi_percent = "The value of pi is approximately %.2f" %
pi

# Printing results
print("F-string formatting:")
print(message_fstring)
print(pi_fstring)

print("\n%-formatting:")
print(message_percent)
print(pi_percent)
```

Preparation (Explanation):

F-string Formatting:

- **Concise Syntax:** F-strings use a simple and intuitive syntax. You enclose variables or expressions in curly braces {} directly within the string.

- **Embedded Expressions:** You can include any valid Python expression within the curly braces. This means you can perform calculations, call functions, or even use conditional expressions within your strings.

- **Formatting Specifiers:** You can control the formatting of the values using format specifiers. For example, :.2f in {pi:.2f} formats pi as a floating-point number with two decimal places.

%-formatting (Legacy):

- **Placeholder Syntax:** %s represents a string placeholder, %d for integers, and %.2f for floating-point numbers with two decimal places.

- **Tuple of Values:** After the string, you provide a tuple (or single value if there's only one placeholder) containing the values to be inserted into the placeholders.

Final Dish (Output):

```
F-string formatting:
Hello, Alice! You are 30 years old.
The value of pi is approximately 3.14

%-formatting:
Hello, Alice! You are 30 years old.
The value of pi is approximately 3.14
```

Why is this important?

- **Dynamic Strings:** String formatting allows you to create strings that change based on variable values, making your code more flexible and reusable.

- **Readability:** F-strings, in particular, offer a highly readable way to embed expressions within strings. The code is closer to the desired output, making it easier to understand.

- **Legacy Code:** While f-strings are preferred in modern Python, you'll still encounter %-formatting in older codebases. Understanding both styles helps you read and maintain a wider range of Python projects.

Key Points:

- F-strings are generally faster and more readable than %-formatting.

- Use format specifiers (like :.2f) to control the precision and appearance of numbers.

- Explore the Python documentation for more advanced string formatting techniques.

4. String Indexing & Slicing:

Recipe 16: Accessing String Characters by Index

Ingredients (Code):

```python
# Python
word = "Python"

# Accessing individual characters
first_letter = word[0]        # Indexing starts at 0
second_letter = word[1]
last_letter = word[-1]        # Negative indices start
from the end

print(f"First letter: {first_letter}")
print(f"Second letter: {second_letter}")
print(f"Last letter: {last_letter}")
```

Preparation (Explanation):

1. **Indexing:**

   - Strings are sequences of characters, and each character has a position within the string, called its index.

   - In Python, indexing starts at 0. So the first character in the string word has the index 0, the second character has index 1, and so on.

   - You can access individual characters by placing their index in square brackets after the string variable.

2. **Positive and Negative Indices:**

   - **Positive Indices:** Count from the beginning of the string, starting at 0.

     - word[0] gives you the first letter ("P").

- word[1] gives you the second letter ("y").

- **Negative Indices:** Count from the end of the string, starting at -1.

  - word[-1] gives you the last letter ("n").

  - word[-2] gives you the second-to-last letter ("o").

Final Dish (Output):

```
First letter: P
Second letter: y
Last letter: n
```

Why is this important?

- **String Manipulation:** Indexing is fundamental for working with individual characters within a string. You can use it to extract specific letters, check for certain characters, or modify parts of a string.

- **Pattern Matching:** Indexing allows you to search for specific patterns or sequences of characters within a string.

- **Error Handling:** Be careful when using indices! If you try to access an index that is out of range (too large or too small), Python will raise an IndexError.

Recipe 17: Slicing Strings (Getting Substrings)

Ingredients (Code):

```
# Python
text = "Python is a powerful programming language."

# Basic slicing
first_word = text[0:6]  # Start at index 0, up to (but
not including) index 6
last_word = text[29:]  # Start at index 29, go to the
end
middle_words = text[7:29] # Start at index 7, up to (but
not including) index 29

print(f"First word: {first_word}")
print(f"Last word: {last_word}")
print(f"Middle words: {middle_words}")


# Slicing with steps
every_other_char = text[::2]  # Start at the beginning,
go to the end, step by 2
reverse_text = text[::-1]  # Reverse the string by
using a negative step

print(f"Every other character: {every_other_char}")
print(f"Reversed text: {reverse_text}")
```

Preparation (Explanation):

1. **Basic Slicing [start:stop]:**

    - You can extract a portion of a string (a substring) using slicing. The syntax is string[start:stop].

    - start is the index where the substring begins (inclusive).

    - stop is the index where the substring ends (exclusive - the character at this index is *not* included).

    - If you omit start, it defaults to the beginning of the string (index 0).

- If you omit stop, it defaults to the end of the string.

2. **Slicing with Steps [start:stop:step]:**

   - You can also include a step value to specify how many characters to skip between each extracted character.

   - A positive step moves forward through the string, while a negative step moves backward.

   - text[::2] means "start at the beginning, go to the end, and take every other character."

   - text[::-1] means "start at the end, go to the beginning (in reverse), and take every character" – effectively reversing the string.

Final Dish (Output):

```
First word: Python
Last word: language.
Middle words: is a powerful programming
Every other character: Pto sapoeflpormiglnug
Reversed text: .egaugnal gnimmargorp lufrewop a si
nohtyP
```

Why is this important?

- **Extracting Information:** Slicing allows you to isolate specific parts of a string, such as words, phrases, or characters.

- **Data Cleaning:** You can use slicing to remove unwanted characters or substrings from text data.

- **Text Transformations:** Slicing enables you to manipulate text in various ways, like reversing strings or extracting alternating characters.

- **Performance:** Slicing is generally efficient, making it a good choice for working with large strings.

Recipe 18: Reverse Indexing

Ingredients (Code):

```python
# Python
text = "Python"

# Reverse Indexing
last_letter = text[-1]
second_last_letter = text[-2]
third_last_letter = text[-3]

print(f"Last letter: {last_letter}")
print(f"Second to last letter: {second_last_letter}")
print(f"Third to last letter: {third_last_letter}")
```

Preparation (Explanation):

1. **Negative Indices:**

    - In Python, you can access elements of a sequence (like a string) from the end using negative indices.

    - The last element has index -1, the second-to-last has index -2, and so on.

    - This is especially useful when you don't know the exact length of the string but want to access elements relative to the end.

2. **Accessing Elements:**

    - text[-1] gives you the last letter ("n").

    - text[-2] gives you the second-to-last letter ("o").

    - text[-3] gives you the third-to-last letter ("h").

Final Dish (Output):

```
Last letter: n
Second to last letter: o
Third to last letter: h
```

Why is this important?

- **Accessing from the End:** Reverse indexing allows you to easily grab characters from the end of a string without having to calculate their position from the beginning. This is particularly handy when dealing with strings of unknown length or when you want to manipulate the end of the string.

- **Slicing:** Reverse indexing also plays a crucial role in string slicing. You can use negative indices to specify the starting and ending points of a slice, counting backward from the end of the string. For example, text[-3:-1] would give you the substring "oh". (See Recipe 17 for more on slicing.)

- **Readability:** In some cases, using negative indices can make your code more intuitive and easier to understand, especially when working with the end of a string.

Recipe 19: Stride in Slicing (Skipping Characters)

Ingredients (Code):

```python
# Python
phrase = "Every good boy does fine."

# Every other character
every_other = phrase[::2]
print(f"Every other character: {every_other}")

# Every third character
every_third = phrase[::3]
print(f"Every third character: {every_third}")

# Reverse every other character
reverse_every_other = phrase[::-2]
print(f"Reverse every other character:
{reverse_every_other}")
```

Preparation (Explanation):

1. **Stride in Slicing [start:stop:step]:**

   - Slicing with a stride allows you to extract characters from a string at regular intervals.

   - The step value determines how many characters to skip between each extracted character.

   - If step is positive, the slicing goes forward; if negative, it goes backward.

2. **Examples:**

   - **phrase[::2]:** Starts at the beginning of the string, goes to the end, and takes every other character (skipping one in between).

   - **phrase[::3]:** Starts at the beginning, goes to the end, and takes every third character (skipping two in between).

- **phrase[::-2]:** Starts at the end, goes backward, and takes every other character. This effectively reverses the string and then takes every other character from the reversed string.

Final Dish (Output):

```
Every other character: Evr od o e ie
Every third character: Eygbdfn
Reverse every other character: .e fd byo oe vrE
```

Why is this important?

- **Pattern Extraction:** Stride in slicing is useful for extracting patterns from strings, such as every other letter or every third word.

- **Data Manipulation:** You can use it to remove specific characters from a string or create modified versions of the text.

- **Reverse Iteration:** Negative strides allow you to iterate through a string in reverse order, which can be helpful for certain types of processing.

- **Conciseness:** Slicing with stride offers a concise way to perform operations that would otherwise require more complex loops and indexing.

Recipe 20: Modifying Strings (Immutability Workaround)

Ingredients (Code):

```python
# Python
original_string = "hello world"

# Incorrect way (doesn't work due to immutability)
# original_string[0] = "H"   # This would raise a
TypeError

# Correct ways to "modify" a string

# 1. Slicing and Concatenation
new_string = "H" + original_string[1:]   # Replace the
first letter
print(new_string)   # Output: Hello world

# 2. Using the `replace()` method
new_string = original_string.replace("l", "L") # Replace
all occurrences of 'l' with 'L'
print(new_string)   # Output: heLLo worLd

# 3. Converting to a list, modifying, and joining back
char_list = list(original_string)
char_list[0] = "H"
new_string = "".join(char_list)
print(new_string)   # Output: Hello world
```

Preparation (Explanation):

1. **Immutability:** Strings in Python are immutable, meaning you cannot directly change their individual characters. Trying to do so (like the commented-out line) will raise a TypeError.

2. **Workarounds:**

   - **Slicing and Concatenation:** Create a new string by combining a slice of the original string with new characters. This is efficient for small changes.

   - **replace() Method:** Create a new string where all occurrences of a specific substring are replaced with another. This is convenient for global replacements.

- **List Conversion:** Convert the string into a list of characters (which is mutable), modify the characters in the list, and then join the list back into a new string. This is flexible but can be less efficient for large strings or numerous modifications.

Final Dish (Output):

```
Hello world
heLLo worLd
Hello world
```

Why is this important?

- **Understanding Immutability:** Recognizing that strings are immutable is crucial for avoiding errors and understanding how Python handles string manipulation.

- **Flexibility:** Python offers multiple ways to effectively "modify" strings, each with its own advantages depending on the specific task.

- **Best Practices:** Choosing the right technique (slicing/concatenation, replace(), or list conversion) can make your code more efficient and maintainable.

Additional Notes:

- In most cases, creating a new string (using slicing, replace(), or list conversion) is the preferred approach, as it aligns with Python's design philosophy of immutability.

- If you need to make numerous modifications to a string, consider using a mutable sequence like a list to

store the characters and then join them into a string at
the end.

5. Advanced String Manipulation:

Recipe 21: Regular Expressions (Searching, Matching, Replacing)

Ingredients (Code):

```python
# Python
import re  # Import the regular expression module

text = "The rain in Spain falls mainly on the plain."

# Searching for a pattern
pattern1 = "ain"
matches = re.findall(pattern1, text)
print(f"Words containing '{pattern1}': {matches}")

# Matching an entire string
pattern2 = "^The.*plain.$" # Match a string starting
with "The" and ending with "plain."
is_match = re.match(pattern2, text)
print(f"Full match: {bool(is_match)}")  # Convert match
object to boolean

# Replacing a pattern
pattern3 = "ai"
new_text = re.sub(pattern3, "**", text)
print(f"Text with '{pattern3}' replaced: {new_text}")
```

Preparation (Explanation):

1. **Import the re Module:** The re (regular expression) module provides powerful tools for working with patterns in text.

2. **Searching with re.findall(pattern, string):**

   - findall returns a list of all non-overlapping matches of the pattern in the string.

   - In our example, it finds all words containing the sequence "ain."

3. **Matching with re.match(pattern, string):**

- match checks if the beginning of the string matches the pattern. It returns a match object if there's a match, or None otherwise.

- The pattern ^The.*plain.$ uses special characters:

  - ^ matches the start of the string.

  - . matches any character (except newline).

  - * means "zero or more repetitions of the previous character."

  - $ matches the end of the string.

4. **Replacing with re.sub(pattern, repl, string):**

  - sub replaces all occurrences of pattern in string with the replacement text repl.

  - In our example, it replaces every "ai" with "**".

Final Dish (Output):

```
Words containing 'ain': ['rain', 'Spain', 'mainly',
'plain']
Full match: True
Text with 'ai' replaced: The r**n **n Sp**n f**lls
m**nly on the pl**n.
```

Why is this important?

- **Pattern Matching:** Regular expressions provide a concise and flexible way to match complex patterns in text, which is crucial for text processing tasks like:

  - **Validation:** Checking if a string matches a specific format (e.g., email address, phone number).

  - **Extraction:** Extracting specific information from unstructured text (e.g., dates, names, URLs).

- **Search and Replace:** Performing targeted replacements in text editors or scripts.

- **Power and Flexibility:** Regular expressions can express a wide range of patterns, from simple character sequences to complex rules involving repetition, alternation, and grouping. This power, however, comes with a slightly steeper learning curve compared to basic string methods.

Recipe 22: String Encoding and Decoding (UTF-8, ASCII)

Ingredients (Code):

```python
# Python
# Text in UTF-8 (supports a wide range of characters)
text_utf8 = "Café Pokémon こんにちは"  # Includes accented
characters and Japanese

# Encode to bytes using UTF-8
bytes_utf8 = text_utf8.encode("utf-8")
print(f"UTF-8 bytes: {bytes_utf8}")

# Decode from bytes back to UTF-8 string
decoded_text_utf8 = bytes_utf8.decode("utf-8")
print(f"Decoded UTF-8: {decoded_text_utf8}")

# Text in ASCII (limited to basic English characters)
text_ascii = "Hello, world!"

# Encode to bytes using ASCII
bytes_ascii = text_ascii.encode("ascii")
print(f"ASCII bytes: {bytes_ascii}")

# Decode from bytes back to ASCII string
decoded_text_ascii = bytes_ascii.decode("ascii")
print(f"Decoded ASCII: {decoded_text_ascii}")

# Attempt to encode non-ASCII characters using ASCII
(will raise UnicodeEncodeError)
# bytes_ascii_error = text_utf8.encode("ascii")
```

Preparation (Explanation):

1. **Character Encodings:**

   - **UTF-8:** A widely used character encoding that can represent virtually any character from any language. It's the default encoding for Python strings.

   - **ASCII:** A much older and simpler encoding limited to basic English characters and a few control codes.

2. **Encoding (encode()):**

- The encode() method converts a string into a sequence of bytes according to a specified encoding.

- text_utf8.encode("utf-8") converts the UTF-8 string to bytes using the UTF-8 encoding.

- text_ascii.encode("ascii") converts the ASCII string to bytes using the ASCII encoding.

3. **Decoding (decode()):**

- The decode() method converts a sequence of bytes back into a string, assuming a specific encoding.

- bytes_utf8.decode("utf-8") decodes the UTF-8 bytes back into the original string.

- bytes_ascii.decode("ascii") decodes the ASCII bytes.

4. **UnicodeEncodeError:**

- The commented-out line demonstrates that trying to encode non-ASCII characters (like the ones in text_utf8) using ASCII will raise a UnicodeEncodeError. This happens because ASCII cannot represent those characters.

Final Dish (Output):

```
UTF-8 bytes: b'Caf\xc3\xa9 Pok\xc3\xa9mon
\xe3\x81\x93\xe3\x82\x93\xe3\x81\xab\xe3\x81\xa1\xe3\x81
\xaf'
Decoded UTF-8: Café Pokémon こんにちは
ASCII bytes: b'Hello, world!'
Decoded ASCII: Hello, world!
```

(The error output for attempting to encode non-ASCII with ASCII is intentionally omitted, but will typically resemble "UnicodeEncodeError: 'ascii' codec can't encode character...")

Why is this important?

- **Text Data Handling:** Encoding and decoding are essential for working with text data in files, network communication, or when interfacing with systems that use different encodings.

- **Unicode Support:** Python's built-in Unicode support and UTF-8 as the default encoding make it well-suited for handling international text.

- **Compatibility:** Understanding encodings helps you avoid errors and ensure that your text is displayed and processed correctly across different platforms and applications.

Recipe 23: Text Justification (Padding, Alignment)

Ingredients (Code):

```python
# Python
text1 = "Left"
text2 = "Center"
text3 = "Right"

width = 20  # Desired width for each line

# Left justification (ljust)
left_justified = text1.ljust(width)
print(f"'{left_justified}'")

# Center justification (center)
center_justified = text2.center(width)
print(f"'{center_justified}'")

# Right justification (rjust)
right_justified = text3.rjust(width)
print(f"'{right_justified}'")

# Custom fill character
custom_justified = text2.center(width, '*')  # Fill with
asterisks
print(f"'{custom_justified}'")
```

Preparation (Explanation):

1. **String Methods for Justification:**

   - **ljust(width, fillchar=' '):** Returns a left-justified version of the string in a field of the given width, padded with fillchar (space by default) on the right.

   - **center(width, fillchar=' '):** Returns a centered version of the string, padded on both sides.

   - **rjust(width, fillchar=' '):** Returns a right-justified version of the string, padded on the left.

2. **Example Usage:**

- We set a desired width of 20 characters for each line.

- We then use the justification methods to align the text strings within this width.

- The custom_justified example shows how to use a different fill character (*).

Final Dish (Output):

```
'Left                '
'       Center       '
'               Right'
'*******Center*******'
```

Why is this important?

- **Presentation:** Text justification is crucial for making text output visually appealing and easy to read. It helps align columns, create headers, and format data in tables.

- **Data Alignment:** In data processing and reporting, you often need to align columns of numbers or text neatly. Justification methods can be used to pad values with spaces or zeros to ensure consistent alignment.

- **Flexibility:** Python's string methods provide flexible ways to control alignment and padding, allowing you to customize the appearance of your text output.

Additional Notes:

- You can use other characters as fillchar for decorative or specific formatting purposes.

- If the string is longer than the specified width, it won't be truncated; it will simply be returned as is.

- For more complex justification scenarios, like text wrapping or full justification, you can use libraries like textwrap or third-party packages.

Recipe 24: Counting Occurrences of Substrings

Ingredients (Code):

```python
# Python
text = "She sells seashells by the seashore. The shells
she sells are seashells, I'm sure."
substring = "shell"

# Method 1: Using count()
count_method1 = text.count(substring)
print(f"Count (method 1): {count_method1}")

# Method 2: Using find() in a loop
count_method2 = 0
index = 0
while index != -1:
    index = text.find(substring, index)   # Start
searching from previous index + 1
    if index != -1:
        count_method2 += 1
        index += len(substring)   # Move to the next
potential starting point
print(f"Count (method 2): {count_method2}")

# Method 3: Using regular expressions (re module)
import re
count_method3 = len(re.findall(substring, text))
print(f"Count (method 3): {count_method3}")
```

Preparation (Explanation):

1. **Method 1: Using count():**

   - The count() method directly returns the number of non-overlapping occurrences of the substring in the text. This is the simplest and most efficient way when you just need the count.

2. **Method 2: Using find() in a loop:**

   - This method manually iterates through the text using find(), which returns the index of the next occurrence of the substring.

- We keep searching until find() returns -1 (meaning no more occurrences found).

- The index variable is updated after each find to start the next search from the character after the previous match.

3. **Method 3: Using Regular Expressions:**

- The re.findall() function from the re module finds all non-overlapping matches of the substring, returning them as a list.

- We use len() to count the number of elements (matches) in the resulting list.

Final Dish (Output):

```
Count (method 1): 4
Count (method 2): 4
Count (method 3): 4
```

Why is this important?

- **Text Analysis:** Counting substring occurrences is essential for various text analysis tasks, such as:

  - Identifying frequent words or phrases

  - Measuring the similarity between documents

  - Detecting specific patterns in text

- **Data Validation:** You can use substring counting to check if a certain word or phrase appears the expected number of times in a text.

- **Performance Considerations:**

  - count() is generally the fastest method when you only need the total count.

- If you need to know the positions of the occurrences or want to do further processing on each match, find() or re.findall() would be more appropriate.

Recipe 25: Palindrome Checker

Ingredients (Code):

```python
# Python
def is_palindrome(word):
  """Checks if a word is a palindrome."""

  # Remove spaces and convert to lowercase for case-
insensitive comparison
  cleaned_word = word.replace(" ", "").lower()

  # Reverse the cleaned word
  reversed_word = cleaned_word[::-1]

  # Compare the original and reversed word
  if cleaned_word == reversed_word:
    return True
  else:
    return False

# Example usage
words_to_check = ["racecar", "level", "hello", "A man, a
plan, a canal: Panama"]

for word in words_to_check:
  if is_palindrome(word):
    print(f"'{word}' is a palindrome")
  else:
    print(f"'{word}' is not a palindrome")
```

Preparation (Explanation):

1. **Function Definition (is_palindrome(word)):**

   - Defines a function named is_palindrome that takes a single argument word (the word to be checked).

2. **Clean the Word:**

   - **word.replace(" ", "").lower():**

     - Removes any spaces from the word (e.g., "race car" becomes "racecar").

     - Converts all characters to lowercase for case-insensitive comparison (e.g., "Racecar" becomes "racecar").

74

3. **Reverse the Word:**

  - **reversed_word = cleaned_word[::-1]:**

    - Slices the cleaned_word with a step of -1, effectively reversing it.

4. **Comparison:**

  - **if cleaned_word == reversed_word:**

    - Compares the original cleaned word with the reversed word.

    - If they are equal, it's a palindrome, and the function returns True.

    - Otherwise, it returns False.

5. **Example Usage:**

  - Creates a list of words to test.

  - Loops through the list, calling is_palindrome() for each word.

  - Prints whether each word is a palindrome or not.

Final Dish (Output):

```
'racecar' is a palindrome
'level' is a palindrome
'hello' is not a palindrome
'A man, a plan, a canal: Panama' is a palindrome
```

Why is this important?

  - **String Manipulation:** Palindrome checking involves manipulating strings by removing spaces and converting to lowercase, and then comparing the original and reversed versions.

- **Problem-Solving:** Palindromes are a classic programming exercise that helps you practice string manipulation, conditional logic, and function design.

6. Collections (Lists, Dictionaries, Tuples, Sets):

Recipe 26: Creating and Accessing Lists

Ingredients (Code):

```python
# Python
# Creating Lists
empty_list = []                        # Empty list
numbers = [1, 2, 3, 4, 5]              # List of numbers
mixed_list = [1, "two", 3.14]  # List with mixed data
types
nested_list = [1, [2, 3], 4]     # Nested list

# Accessing Elements by Index (zero-based)
print(f"First number: {numbers[0]}")        # Access the
first element (index 0)
print(f"Last number: {numbers[-1]}")         # Access the
last element (index -1)
print(f"Element from nested list: {nested_list[1][1]}")
# Access nested element

# Slicing Lists (to get sublists)
print(f"First two numbers: {numbers[:2]}")      # From the
start up to (but excluding) index 2
print(f"Last two numbers: {numbers[-2:]}")    # From the
second-to-last element to the end
print(f"Every other number: {numbers[::2]}") # Start to
end, step by 2

# Checking if an item exists
if 3 in numbers:
    print("3 is in the list")
```

Preparation (Explanation):

1. **Creating Lists:**

    - **[]:** Square brackets are used to define a list.

    - Elements are separated by commas.

    - Lists can contain elements of different data types (even other lists).

2. **Accessing Elements:**

- **Index:** Each element in a list has a position, called its index.

- **Zero-Based Indexing:** In Python, indexing starts at 0, so the first element has index 0, the second has index 1, and so on.

- **Negative Indexing:** You can also access elements from the end using negative indices: -1 for the last element, -2 for the second to last, etc.

- **Syntax:** Use list_name[index] to access an element at a specific index.

3. **Slicing:**

- **Syntax:** list_name[start:stop:step]

- **start:** The index where the slice starts (inclusive, default is 0).

- **stop:** The index where the slice ends (exclusive, default is the length of the list).

- **step:** The number of indices to jump between elements (default is 1).

4. **Membership Test (in):**

- The in operator checks if a value is present in the list. It returns True if found, and False otherwise.

Final Dish (Output):

```
First number: 1
Last number: 5
Element from nested list: 3
First two numbers: [1, 2]
Last two numbers: [4, 5]
Every other number: [1, 3, 5]
3 is in the list
```

Why is this important?

- **Storing Collections:** Lists are essential for storing and organizing multiple related items. They are versatile and can be used for various types of data.

- **Data Manipulation:** You can add, remove, and modify elements in lists, making them dynamic and flexible.

- **Iteration:** Lists are easily iterable, meaning you can process each element one by one using loops.

Recipe 27: List Operations (append(), insert(), remove(), sort(), reverse())

Ingredients (Code):

```python
# Python
numbers = [5, 2, 8, 1, 9]

# append() - Add to the end
numbers.append(6)
print(f"After append: {numbers}")

# insert() - Insert at a specific index
numbers.insert(2, 3)   # Insert 3 at index 2
print(f"After insert: {numbers}")

# remove() - Remove the first occurrence of a value
numbers.remove(8)
print(f"After remove: {numbers}")

# sort() - Sort the list in ascending order (in-place)
numbers.sort()
print(f"After sort: {numbers}")

# reverse() - Reverse the list in-place
numbers.reverse()
print(f"After reverse: {numbers}")
```

Preparation (Explanation):

1. **append(item):**

   - Adds an item to the end of the list.

   - Modifies the list in-place (does not return a new list).

   - In the example, 6 is added to the end of the numbers list.

2. **insert(index, item):**

   - Inserts an item at the specified index.

   - All existing elements from that position onwards are shifted to the right.

- In the example, 3 is inserted at index 2, shifting 8 and subsequent elements.

3. **remove(value):**

  - Removes the first occurrence of the specified value from the list.

  - Raises a ValueError if the value is not found.

  - In the example, the first 8 is removed.

4. **sort():**

  - Sorts the elements of the list in ascending order.

  - Modifies the list in-place.

  - You can also use numbers.sort(reverse=True) to sort in descending order.

5. **reverse():**

  - Reverses the order of elements in the list.

  - Modifies the list in-place.

Final Dish (Output):

```
After append: [5, 2, 8, 1, 9, 6]
After insert: [5, 2, 3, 8, 1, 9, 6]
After remove: [5, 2, 3, 1, 9, 6]
After sort: [1, 2, 3, 5, 6, 9]
After reverse: [9, 6, 5, 3, 2, 1]
```

Why is this important?

- **List Manipulation:** These operations are fundamental for modifying and rearranging elements in lists, which is essential for many programming tasks.

- **Data Organization:** Sorting and reversing are useful for organizing data for display or analysis.

- **In-Place
  Operations:** append(), insert(), sort(), and reverse() m
  odify the original list directly, which is memory-efficient
  for large lists.

Additional Notes:

- **Other Operations:** Lists have many other methods for
  manipulation, including pop(), extend(), clear(), and
  more.

- **Copying Lists:** If you want to make a copy of a list
  without modifying the original, use new_list =
  list.copy() or new_list = list[:].

- **Performance:** Be mindful of the time complexity of list
  operations. For example, inserting or removing elements
  at the beginning of a large list can be slower than
  appending.

Recipe 28: Dictionaries (Key-Value Pairs, Accessing, Modifying)

Ingredients (Code):

```python
# Python
# Creating Dictionaries
person = {'name': 'Alice', 'age': 30, 'city': 'New
York'}  # Using curly braces
empty_dict = {}
# Empty dictionary

# Accessing Values
name = person['name']
age = person.get('age')        # get() is safer for non-
existent keys
city = person.get('country', 'Unknown')  # Default value
if key not found

print(f"Name: {name}")
print(f"Age: {age}")
print(f"City: {city}")


# Modifying Dictionaries
person['age'] = 31             # Modify an existing value
person['occupation'] = 'Software Engineer'  # Add a new
key-value pair

# Deleting Items
del person['city']

# Dictionary Membership (in, not in)
if 'age' in person:
    print("Person has an age entry")

print("\nUpdated Person:", person)
```

Preparation (Explanation):

1. **Creating Dictionaries:**

   - **Curly Braces:** Define dictionaries using curly braces {}.

   - **Key-Value Pairs:** Dictionaries store data in key-value pairs. Keys are unique identifiers (like words in a dictionary), and values are the associated data. Separate key-value pairs with commas.

83

2. **Accessing Values:**

- **Square Brackets:** Use dictionary_name[key] to retrieve the value associated with a specific key. If the key doesn't exist, you'll get a KeyError.

- **get() Method:** The get() method provides a safer way to access values. It returns the value if the key exists, otherwise, it returns None (or a default value you specify).

3. **Modifying Dictionaries:**

- **Assignment:** Assign a new value to an existing key using dictionary_name[key] = new_value.

- **Adding New Keys:** Create a new key-value pair by assigning a value to a new key that doesn't exist yet.

- **Deleting Items:** Use the del statement with del dictionary_name[key] to remove a key-value pair.

4. **Membership Test (in, not in):**

- Checks whether a specific key exists in the dictionary.

Final Dish (Output):

```
Name: Alice
Age: 30
City: Unknown

Updated Person: {'name': 'Alice', 'age': 31,
'occupation': 'Software Engineer'}
Person has an age entry
```

Why is this important?

- **Flexible Data Storage:** Dictionaries provide a flexible way to store and organize data that has a natural key-value structure, such as user profiles, configuration settings, or product catalogs.

- **Fast Lookup:** Dictionaries are optimized for quickly looking up values by their keys, making them efficient for retrieval operations.

- **Data Manipulation:** You can easily modify and update dictionary contents by adding, removing, or changing key-value pairs.

Recipe 29: Tuple Operations (Packing, Unpacking, Indexing)

Ingredients (Code):

```python
# Python
# Packing: Creating a tuple implicitly
point = 3, 5  # Parentheses are optional for packing
print(f"Point: {point}, Type: {type(point)}")

# Unpacking: Assigning tuple values to variables
x, y = point
print(f"x: {x}, y: {y}")

# Packing and Unpacking in one line
x, y = (10, 20)
print(f"New x: {x}, New y: {y}")

# Indexing
coordinates = (12, -5, 8)
first_coordinate = coordinates[0]
last_coordinate = coordinates[-1]

print(f"First coordinate: {first_coordinate}")
print(f"Last coordinate: {last_coordinate}")
```

Preparation (Explanation):

1. **Packing:**

   - **Implicit Creation:** Tuples can be created implicitly by simply separating values with commas. The parentheses () are optional but often used for clarity.

   - In the example, point = 3, 5 creates a tuple with two elements: 3 and 5.

2. **Unpacking:**

   - **Assigning to Variables:** You can "unpack" a tuple by assigning its elements to individual variables. The number of variables should match the number of elements in the tuple.

86

- In the example, x, y = point assigns 3 to x and 5 to y.

- **One-Liner:** You can combine packing and unpacking into a single line to create and immediately assign values from a tuple.

3. **Indexing:**

   - **Zero-Based:** Tuples, like lists, are indexed from zero.

   - **Accessing Elements:** Use square brackets [] with the index to access individual elements within the tuple.

   - **Negative Indexing:** You can also use negative indices to access elements from the end, e.g., [-1] for the last element.

Final Dish (Output):

```
Point: (3, 5), Type: <class 'tuple'>
x: 3, y: 5
New x: 10, New y: 20
First coordinate: 12
Last coordinate: 8
```

Why is this important?

- **Immutability:** Tuples are immutable, meaning their values cannot be changed after creation. This makes them suitable for representing fixed data structures like coordinates, dates, or RGB color values.

- **Data Integrity:** The immutability of tuples helps prevent accidental modifications, making your code more reliable.

- **Concise Syntax:** The packing and unpacking syntax provides a concise and elegant way to work with multiple values simultaneously.

- **Multiple Return Values:** Functions can return tuples, allowing you to effectively return multiple values.

Recipe 30: Set Operations (Union, Intersection, Difference)

Ingredients (Code):

```python
# Python
# Creating sets
set1 = {1, 2, 3, 4, 5}
set2 = {4, 5, 6, 7, 8}

# Union (|) - Combine all unique elements
union_set = set1 | set2
print(f"Union: {union_set}")

# Intersection (&) - Find common elements
intersection_set = set1 & set2
print(f"Intersection: {intersection_set}")

# Difference (-) - Find elements in set1 but not in set2
difference_set1 = set1 - set2
print(f"Difference (set1 - set2): {difference_set1}")

# Difference (-) - Find elements in set2 but not in set1
difference_set2 = set2 - set1
print(f"Difference (set2 - set1): {difference_set2}")

# Symmetric Difference (^) - Find unique elements in
either set
symmetric_difference_set = set1 ^ set2
print(f"Symmetric Difference:
{symmetric_difference_set}")
```

Preparation (Explanation):

1. **Creating Sets:**

   - Sets are defined using curly braces {} or the set() constructor.

   - Sets contain unique, unordered elements.

2. **Set Operations:**

   - **Union (| or union())**

     - Combines all unique elements from two or more sets into a new set.

- **Intersection (& or intersection()):**

  - Creates a new set containing only the elements that are common to both sets.

- **Difference (- or difference()):**

  - Creates a new set containing the elements that are in the first set but not in the second set.

- **Symmetric Difference (^ or symmetric_difference()):**

  - Creates a new set containing all the unique elements that are in either of the sets, but not in both.

Final Dish (Output):

```
Union: {1, 2, 3, 4, 5, 6, 7, 8}
Intersection: {4, 5}
Difference (set1 - set2): {1, 2, 3}
Difference (set2 - set1): {8, 6, 7}
Symmetric Difference: {1, 2, 3, 6, 7, 8}
```

Why is this important?

- **Removing Duplicates:** Sets automatically remove duplicate elements, making them perfect for tasks where uniqueness is required.

- **Data Comparison:** Set operations are handy for comparing collections of data to find commonalities, differences, or unique items.

- **Membership Testing:** You can efficiently check if an item exists in a set using the in and not in operators.

- **Mathematical Set Operations:** Python sets support many mathematical set operations like subsets, supersets, and disjoint sets, which are useful in various mathematical and computational problems.

7. Boolean Operations & Control Flow:

Recipe 31: Boolean Values (True, False) and Operators (and, or, not)

Ingredients (Code):

```python
# Python
# Boolean values
is_raining = True
is_sunny = False

# Logical AND operator
if is_raining and is_sunny:
    print("It's a miracle! Raining and sunny at the same time.")
else:
    print("Either it's raining or it's sunny, or it's neither.")

# Logical OR operator
if is_raining or is_sunny:
    print("The weather is interesting today.")
else:
    print("The weather is quite dull.")

# Logical NOT operator
if not is_raining:
    print("No rain today!")
else:
    print("Bring your umbrella.")

# Combining operators
is_cold = True
if is_raining and not is_sunny and is_cold:
    print("It's a cold, rainy day. Better stay inside!")
```

Preparation (Explanation):

1. **Boolean Values:**

   • Boolean values are used to represent truth values: True or False. They are fundamental for decision-making and control flow in programming.

2. **Logical Operators:**

- and (Logical AND): True only if both conditions are True.

- or (Logical OR): True if at least one condition is True.

- not (Logical NOT): Reverses the truth value of a boolean expression (True becomes False, and False becomes True).

3. **Examples:**

- is_raining and is_sunny: Evaluates to True only if both is_raining and is_sunny are True. In most cases, this would be False.

- is_raining or is_sunny: Evaluates to True if either (or both) is_raining or is_sunny are True.

- not is_raining: Evaluates to True if is_raining is False, and vice-versa.

Final Dish (Output):

```
Either it's raining or it's sunny, or it's neither.
The weather is interesting today.
Bring your umbrella.
It's a cold, rainy day. Better stay inside!
```

Why is this important?

- **Decision Making:** Boolean values and logical operators are essential for creating conditional statements (if, elif, else) that control the flow of your program based on different conditions.

- **Truth Testing:** You can use boolean expressions to evaluate the truthiness of different conditions.

- **Combining Conditions:** Logical operators let you combine multiple conditions to create more complex expressions.

- **Logical Negation:** The not operator is useful for inverting conditions and handling cases where you want to check if something is not true.

Recipe 32: If, Elif, and Else Statements

Ingredients (Code):

```python
# Python
temperature = 18   # In degrees Celsius

if temperature > 30:
    print("It's a hot day. Drink plenty of water!")
elif temperature >= 20:   # Temperature between 20 and 30
(inclusive)
    print("It's a pleasant day.")
elif temperature >= 10:   # Temperature between 10 and 19
(inclusive)
    print("It's a bit chilly.")
else:                           # Temperature below 10
    print("It's cold. Wear a warm coat!")
```

Preparation (Explanation):

1. **Conditional Statements:**

   - if, elif, and else allow you to execute different blocks of code based on whether certain conditions are met.

   - if: The first condition that is evaluated. If it's True, its code block is executed, and the rest are skipped.

   - elif: "Else if." A series of additional conditions to check if the previous if or elif conditions were False.

   - else: The final "catch-all" condition. Its code block executes only if all previous conditions were False.

2. **Example:**

   - We set a temperature variable to 18 degrees Celsius.

   - The if statement checks if it's greater than 30. Since it's not, it moves to the first elif.

95

- The elif checks if it's 20 or above. It's not, so it moves to the next elif.

- The second elif checks if it's 10 or above. This condition is True, so its print statement is executed.

- The else statement is skipped because a previous condition was met.

Final Dish (Output):

```
It's a bit chilly.
```

Why is this important?

- **Decision Making:** Conditional statements are the core of decision-making in programming. They let your programs react to different inputs and situations.

- **Flexibility:** You can chain multiple elif blocks to handle a wide range of possibilities.

- **Default Behavior:** The else block provides a default action to take when none of the other conditions are met.

- **Readability:** Using if, elif, and else makes your code easier to read and understand, as the logic flow is clearly defined.

Key Points:

- **Indentation:** The code blocks under if, elif, and else are indented to indicate that they belong to that specific condition.

- **Order Matters:** Conditions are checked from top to bottom. Once a condition is met, the rest are ignored.

Recipe 33: Comparison Operators (==, !=, <, >, <=, >=)

Ingredients (Code):

```python
# Python
x = 10
y = 5

# Equality (==)
print(f"{x} == {y}: {x == y}")

# Inequality (!=)
print(f"{x} != {y}: {x != y}")

# Less than (<)
print(f"{x} < {y}: {x < y}")

# Greater than (>)
print(f"{x} > {y}: {x > y}")

# Less than or equal to (<=)
print(f"{x} <= {y}: {x <= y}")

# Greater than or equal to (>=)
print(f"{x} >= {y}: {x >= y}")
```

Preparation (Explanation):

1. **Comparison Operators:**

   - These operators compare two values and return a Boolean result (True or False) based on the relationship between the values.

2. **Operators:**

   - == (Equal to): Checks if two values are equal.

   - != (Not equal to): Checks if two values are not equal.

   - < (Less than): Checks if the left operand is less than the right operand.

- > (Greater than): Checks if the left operand is greater than the right operand.

- <= (Less than or equal to): Checks if the left operand is less than or equal to the right operand.

- >= (Greater than or equal to): Checks if the left operand is greater than or equal to the right operand.

3. **Example:**

- In the code, we have two variables, x (value 10) and y (value 5).

- Each comparison operator is used to compare x and y, and the result (True or False) is printed along with the comparison statement.

Final Dish (Output):

```
10 == 5: False
10 != 5: True
10 < 5: False
10 > 5: True
10 <= 5: False
10 >= 5: True
```

Why is this important?

- **Decision Making:** Comparison operators are the foundation of decision-making in programming. They are used in conditional statements (if, elif, else) to control the flow of your program based on whether certain conditions are met.

- **Sorting and Filtering:** Comparison operators are used to sort data in ascending or descending order and to filter data based on specific criteria.

- **Data Validation:** You can use comparison operators to validate user input and ensure that data meets certain requirements.

- **Logical Expressions:** Comparison operators can be combined with logical operators (and, or, not) to build complex logical expressions.

Recipe 34: Nested Conditional Statements

Ingredients (Code):

```python
# Python
x = 15
y = 25

if x > 10:
    print("x is greater than 10")
    if y > 20:
        print("y is greater than 20")
    else:
        print("y is less than or equal to 20")
else:
    print("x is less than or equal to 10")
    if y < 15:
        print("y is less than 15")
    else:
        print("y is greater than or equal to 15")
```

Preparation (Explanation):

1. **Nested if Statements:**

   - A nested if statement is an if statement placed inside another if statement. It allows you to create multiple levels of decision-making in your code.

   - The inner if statement is only executed if the outer if statement's condition is True.

2. **Example:**

   - Outer if: Checks if x is greater than 10. Since it is (15 > 10), the print statement inside this block executes, and then the code moves to the inner if statement.

   - Inner if: Checks if y is greater than 20. Since it is (25 > 20), the print statement inside this inner block executes. If it wasn't, the else block of the inner if would run.

- The second set of nested if-else statements within the else block of the outer if are skipped because the outer if condition was True.

Final Dish (Output):

```
x is greater than 10
y is greater than 20
```

Why is this important?

- **Complex Logic:** Nested conditionals are essential for handling complex logic where decisions depend on multiple factors.

- **Organization:** They can help you organize your code into more manageable and readable chunks.

- **Flexibility:** You can have as many levels of nesting as needed to model intricate decision trees.

Key Points:

- **Indentation:** Proper indentation is crucial to indicate which blocks of code belong to which if, elif, or else conditions.

- **Readability:** While nested conditionals are powerful, be mindful of overusing them. Too many levels of nesting can make your code difficult to understand and maintain. Consider refactoring into smaller functions or using different control structures if the logic becomes overly complex.

Recipe 35: Ternary Operator (x if condition else y)

Ingredients (Code):

```python
# Python
age = 25
status = "Adult" if age >= 18 else "Minor"
print(f"You are an {status}.")

number = -7
sign = "Positive" if number > 0 else "Negative" if
number < 0 else "Zero"
print(f"The number {number} is {sign}.")
```

Preparation (Explanation):

1. **Ternary Operator Syntax:**

   - The ternary operator is a concise way to write a conditional expression in a single line. The syntax is:

   ```python
   #Python
   result = [on_true] if [condition] else [on_false]
   ```
   - condition: A Boolean expression that is evaluated to True or False.

   - on_true: The value returned if the condition is True.

   - on_false: The value returned if the condition is False.

2. **Examples:**

   - **First Example:**

     - age >= 18: The condition checks if the age is 18 or older.

     - "Adult": The value returned if the condition is True.

- "Minor": The value returned if the condition is False.

- **Second Example:**

  - This example demonstrates nested ternary operators for multiple conditions.

  - It checks if number is positive, negative, or zero and assigns the appropriate string to the sign variable.

Final Dish (Output):

```
You are an Adult.
The number -7 is Negative.
```

Why is this important?

- **Conciseness:** The ternary operator provides a concise way to write simple conditional assignments. It can replace a multi-line if-else statement with a single line, making your code more compact and readable.

- **Readability:** When used appropriately (for simple conditions), the ternary operator can improve code readability by expressing the logic more directly.

- **Inline Expressions:** You can use the ternary operator within larger expressions, offering flexibility in how you construct conditional logic.

Key Points:

- **Overuse Caution:** Avoid using nested ternary operators excessively, as it can quickly make your code hard to read. If the logic becomes complex, an if-else statement is often a better choice.

- **Alternative:** Python also has conditional expressions using the and-or syntax, which can be an alternative in some cases (but may not always be as readable).

8. Loops (For & While):

Recipe 36: For Loops (Iterating Over Sequences)

Ingredients (Code):

```python
# Python
# Iterating over a string
message = "Hello, world!"
for char in message:
    print(char)

# Iterating over a list
numbers = [1, 3, 5, 7, 9]
for num in numbers:
    print(num * 2)  # Print each number doubled

# Iterating over a range of numbers
for i in range(1, 6):  # Start at 1, up to (but not
including) 6
    print(i)
```

Preparation (Explanation):

1. **For Loop Structure:**

   - **for variable in sequence:**

     - **variable:** A temporary variable that takes on each value in the sequence during each iteration.

     - **in:** The keyword indicating iteration over a sequence.

     - **sequence:** The collection of items you want to iterate over
       (strings, lists, tuples, ranges, etc.).

2. **Examples:**

   - **Iterating over a string:**

- The loop assigns each character in the string message to the variable char and then prints it.

- **Iterating over a list:**

  - The loop assigns each number in the list numbers to the variable num and then prints the result of doubling that number.

- **Iterating over a range:**

  - The range(1, 6) function generates a sequence of numbers from 1 to 5 (inclusive). The loop variable i takes on each of these values, and they are printed.

Final Dish (Output):

```
H
e
l
l
o
,

w
o
r
l
d
!
2
6
10
14
18
1
2
3
4
5
```

Why is this important?

- **Repetitive Tasks:** For loops are excellent for automating repetitive tasks that involve processing each item in a sequence.

- **Sequence Traversal:** They provide a straightforward way to access and work with individual elements within a sequence.

- **Flexibility:** Python's for loops work with a wide variety of sequences, making them a versatile tool for different scenarios.

Key Points:

- The variable in a for loop doesn't have to be declared beforehand.

- You can iterate over lists, tuples, strings, and even custom objects that support iteration (like dictionaries).

- The range() function is very useful for generating sequences of numbers.

- The for loop automatically handles the iteration process, making your code cleaner and less error-prone.

Recipe 37: While Loops (Condition-Based Iteration)

Ingredients (Code):

```python
# Python
# Simple countdown
countdown = 5
while countdown > 0:
  print(f"Counting down: {countdown}")
  countdown -= 1  # Equivalent to countdown = countdown - 1
print("Blastoff!")

# User input loop
message = ""
while message != "quit":
  message = input("Enter a message ('quit' to exit): ")
  if message != "quit":
    print(f"You said: {message}")
print("Exiting loop...")

# Guessing game
import random
secret_number = random.randint(1, 10)
guess = 0
while guess != secret_number:
  guess = int(input("Guess a number between 1 and 10: "))
  if guess < secret_number:
    print("Too low!")
  elif guess > secret_number:
    print("Too high!")
print(f"You guessed it! The number was {secret_number}")
```

Preparation (Explanation):

1. **While Loop Structure:**

   - **while condition:**

     - condition: A Boolean expression (evaluates to True or False).

     - The loop continues to execute the code block as long as the condition remains True.

2. **Examples:**

- **Countdown:** The loop runs as long as countdown is greater than 0, printing the countdown value and then decrementing it.

- **User Input Loop:** The loop continues until the user enters the word "quit." It prompts for input, prints the message (unless it's "quit"), and then checks the condition again.

- **Guessing Game:** The loop runs until the user guesses the correct secret_number. It provides feedback ("Too low!" or "Too high!") to guide the user.

Final Dish (Output):

```
Counting down: 5
Counting down: 4
Counting down: 3
Counting down: 2
Counting down: 1
Blastoff!
Enter a message ('quit' to exit): hello
You said: hello
Enter a message ('quit' to exit): Python is awesome
You said: Python is awesome
Enter a message ('quit' to exit): quit
Exiting loop...

Guess a number between 1 and 10: 5
Too high!
Guess a number between 1 and 10: 2
Too low!
Guess a number between 1 and 10: 3
You guessed it! The number was 3
```

Why is this important?

- **Indefinite Iteration:** Unlike for loops, which iterate over a known sequence, while loops run for an indefinite number of times, as long as a condition is met. This is useful when you don't know how many iterations you'll need in advance.

- **User Input and Interaction:** while loops are commonly used to create interactive programs that respond to user input, as in the input loop example.

- **Repetition with a Condition:** while loops excel at tasks where you need to repeat actions until a specific goal is achieved, such as the guessing game example.

Recipe 38: Break and Continue Statements

Ingredients (Code):

```python
# Python
# Break Statement
for num in range(1, 11):
    if num == 7:
        print("Found the lucky number 7!")
        break  # Exit the loop completely
    print(num)

print("-" * 10) # Add separator

# Continue Statement
for num in range(1, 11):
    if num % 2 == 0:  # Check if num is even
        continue  # Skip the rest of this iteration and
move to the next
    print(num)  # Only odd numbers are printed
```

Preparation (Explanation):

1. **break Statement:**

   - **Purpose:** The break statement immediately terminates the loop it's inside. Execution continues with the code after the loop.

   - **Example (Lucky Number):** The for loop iterates through numbers 1 to 10. When it reaches 7, the if condition is met, and the break statement is executed. This causes the loop to end, and the "Blastoff!" message is printed.

2. **continue Statement:**

   - **Purpose:** The continue statement skips the rest of the current iteration of the loop and jumps to the beginning of the next iteration.

   - **Example (Odd Numbers):** The for loop iterates through numbers 1 to 10. If a number is even (divisible by 2), the continue statement is encountered. This causes the print(num) line to be skipped for even numbers, and only odd numbers are printed.

Final Dish (Output):

```
1
2
3
4
5
6
Found the lucky number 7!
----------
1
3
5
7
9
```

Why is this important?

- **Loop Control:** These statements provide finer control over the execution flow of loops.

- **Early Termination:** break is useful when you want to stop a loop prematurely based on a certain condition (e.g., when you find what you're looking for).

- **Filtering:** continue helps filter out unwanted items during iteration, allowing you to focus on specific elements (e.g., only processing odd numbers).

Key Points:

- Both break and continue work with both for and while loops.

- Using them wisely can lead to more concise and efficient code.

Recipe 39: Nested Loops (Pattern Printing, Matrix Manipulation)

Ingredients (Code):

```python
# Python
# Pattern Printing
rows = 5
for i in range(1, rows + 1):
    for j in range(i):
        print("*", end="")  # Print * without a newline
    print()  # Print a newline after each row

print("-" * 10) # Add separator


# Matrix Manipulation
matrix = [[1, 2, 3],
          [4, 5, 6],
          [7, 8, 9]]

# Accessing elements
print(f"Element at row 1, column 2: {matrix[1][2]}")

# Iterating through rows and columns
for row in matrix:
    for element in row:
        print(element, end=" ")
    print()
```

Preparation (Explanation):

1. Pattern Printing:

- **Nested For Loops:** The outer for loop iterates over the rows. For each row, the inner for loop iterates i times (where i is the current row number).

- **Printing Stars:** The inner loop prints an asterisk ("*") for each iteration. The end="" argument prevents automatic newlines, so asterisks are printed on the same line.

- **Newline After Each Row:** After the inner loop completes, print() without arguments is used to move to the next line.

113

2. Matrix Manipulation:

- **2D List:** A matrix is represented as a list of lists, where each inner list is a row.

- **Accessing Elements:** You can access individual elements using two indices: matrix[row_index][column_index]. Note that indexing starts at 0.

- **Nested Loops for Iteration:** Nested loops are perfect for iterating over matrices. The outer loop iterates over rows, and the inner loop iterates over elements within each row.

Final Dish (Output):

```
*
* *
* * *
* * * *
* * * * *
----------
Element at row 1, column 2: 6
1 2 3
4 5 6
7 8 9
```

Why is this important?

- **Pattern Generation:** Nested loops are a fundamental tool for creating various text-based patterns, from simple triangles to complex geometric shapes.

- **Matrix Operations:** Matrices are widely used in mathematics, physics, engineering, and data science. Nested loops provide a way to perform operations on matrix elements, like adding, multiplying, or transforming them.

- **Image Processing:** Nested loops are used to process image data, where each pixel is represented as an element in a 2D matrix.

Recipe 40: Infinite Loops (And How to Avoid Them)

Ingredients (Code):

```python
# Python
# Example 1: Unintentional Infinite Loop
# while True:   # This loop will run forever (commented
out to prevent it)
#    print("This loop will never end!")

# Example 2: Intentional Infinite Loop with a Break
Condition
while True:
  number = int(input("Enter a positive number (or 0 to
exit): "))
  if number == 0:
    break
  print(f"You entered: {number}")
print("Loop exited.")

# Example 3: Infinite Loop with a Counter and Break
Condition
counter = 0
while True:
  counter += 1
  print(f"Counter: {counter}")
  if counter >= 10:
    break
print("Loop stopped after 10 iterations.")
```

Preparation (Explanation):

1. **Example 1: Unintentional Infinite Loop**

    - The commented-out code demonstrates an infinite while loop. The condition True is always true, so the loop never ends. This can freeze your program or consume system resources. Avoid this!

2. **Example 2: Intentional Infinite Loop with a Break Condition**

    - This loop is designed to run indefinitely until the user enters the number 0.

- The break statement inside the if block terminates the loop when the condition number == 0 becomes True.

3. **Example 3: Infinite Loop with a Counter and Break Condition**

- This loop also runs indefinitely, but it uses a counter variable to keep track of the iterations.

- The break statement exits the loop when the counter reaches 10.

Final Dish (Output):

```
(Example 1 would run forever if uncommented)

Enter a positive number (or 0 to exit): 5
You entered: 5
Enter a positive number (or 0 to exit): 22
You entered: 22
Enter a positive number (or 0 to exit): 0
Loop exited.

Counter: 1
Counter: 2
Counter: 3
Counter: 4
Counter: 5
Counter: 6
Counter: 7
Counter: 8
Counter: 9
Counter: 10
Loop stopped after 10 iterations.
```

Why is this important?

- **Avoiding Crashes:** Infinite loops can cause your program to hang or crash if they are not handled properly.

- **Resource Management:** They can also consume excessive system resources, like CPU time and memory.

- **Controlled Repetition:** Intentional infinite loops can be used to create interactive programs or those that run continuously until a specific condition is met, but they should always have a well-defined exit strategy using a break statement.

Key Points:

- **Always have an exit condition:** Ensure that your while loops have a way to break out, either by the user providing input, a counter reaching a limit, or some other condition becoming true.

- **Check for unexpected conditions:** Test your loops with various inputs to make sure they don't become infinite unintentionally.

- **Debugging:** If you encounter an infinite loop, use debugging tools or print statements to track the loop's progress and identify the cause of the issue.

9. Functions:

Recipe 41: Defining and Calling Functions

Ingredients (Code):

```python
# Python
# Function definition
def greet(name):
    """This function greets the person passed in as a
parameter"""
    print(f"Hello, {name}!")


# Function call
greet("Alice")  # Call the function with the argument
"Alice"
greet("Bob")    # Call the function again with a
different argument

# Function with a return value
def add_numbers(a, b):
    """This function adds two numbers and returns the
result"""
    sum = a + b
    return sum


# Calling the function and storing the result
result = add_numbers(5, 3)
print(f"The sum is: {result}")
```

Preparation (Explanation):

1. **Function Definition (def):**

   - **def greet(name)::**

     - This line defines a function named greet.

     - The name inside the parentheses is a parameter. It's a placeholder for a value that will be passed to the function when it's called.

- The colon : indicates the start of the function's code block.

- **Docstring:**

  - The text enclosed in triple quotes (""""..."""") is a docstring. It serves as a documentation for the function, explaining its purpose and usage.

- **Function Body:**

  - The code within the function's block defines what the function does. In this case, it prints a greeting using the name parameter.

2. **Function Call:**

- **greet("Alice"):**

  - This line calls the greet function.

  - The string "Alice" is passed as an argument to the function. This value is assigned to the name parameter inside the function.

3. **Functions with Return Values:**

- The add_numbers function takes two parameters (a and b).

- It calculates their sum and stores it in the variable sum.

- The return statement sends this sum value back to the place where the function was called.

4. **Using Return Values:**

- **result = add_numbers(5, 3):** The function is called with arguments 5 and 3. The returned value (8) is stored in the variable result.

- This result can then be used in other parts of your code.

Final Dish (Output):

```
Hello, Alice!
Hello, Bob!
The sum is: 8
```

Why is this important?

- **Code Reusability:** Functions allow you to write a block of code once and use it multiple times with different inputs.

- **Modularity:** Functions break down complex tasks into smaller, manageable parts, making your code easier to understand and maintain.

- **Abstraction:** Functions hide the details of how something is done, letting you focus on what the function does. This improves readability and reduces the risk of errors.

Recipe 42: Function Arguments (Positional, Keyword)

Ingredients (Code):

```python
# Python
def describe_pet(animal_type, pet_name):
    """Displays information about a pet."""
    print(f"\nI have a {animal_type}.")
    print(f"My {animal_type}'s name is
{pet_name.title()}.")

# Call the function using positional arguments (order
matters)
describe_pet("hamster", "harry")

# Call the function using keyword arguments (order
doesn't matter)
describe_pet(pet_name="willie", animal_type="dog")
```

Preparation (Explanation):

1. **Function Definition:**

   - The describe_pet function takes two parameters: animal_type and pet_name.

2. **Positional Arguments:**

   - When calling the function using positional arguments, you must provide the arguments in the same order as the parameters are defined in the function's definition.

   - For example, describe_pet("hamster", "harry") passes "hamster" to the animal_type parameter and "harry" to the pet_name parameter.

3. **Keyword Arguments:**

   - Keyword arguments explicitly associate a value with a parameter by name.

- The order of keyword arguments doesn't matter.

- For example, describe_pet(pet_name="willie", animal_type="dog") is equivalent to the previous call.

Final Dish (Output):

```
I have a hamster.
My hamster's name is Harry.

I have a dog.
My dog's name is Willie.
```

Why is this important?

- **Flexibility:** Keyword arguments provide flexibility by allowing you to change the order of arguments when calling functions, making your code more readable and less prone to errors when there are many arguments.

- **Clarity:** Keyword arguments make your code self-documenting. It's clear which value is being assigned to which parameter.

- **Default Values:** You can set default values for parameters (e.g., pet_name="Buddy"). If the caller doesn't provide a value for that argument, the default is used. (See the next recipe for more on this!)

Key Points:

- **Mixing Positional and Keyword Arguments:** You can mix positional and keyword arguments, but positional arguments must come before keyword arguments in the function call.

- **Readability:** Prefer keyword arguments for functions with multiple parameters or when the order of arguments might not be obvious.

Recipe 43: Return Values

Ingredients (Code):

```python
# Python
# Function with a return value
def square(number):
    """Calculates the square of a number."""
    result = number * number
    return result

# Get input from the user
user_number = float(input("Enter a number: "))

# Call the function and store the returned value
squared_value = square(user_number)

# Print the result
print(f"The square of {user_number} is {squared_value}")


# Function with multiple return values
def get_name_and_age():
    """Prompts the user for name and age, and returns them
as a tuple."""
    name = input("Enter your name: ")
    age = int(input("Enter your age: "))
    return name, age  # Return multiple values as a tuple

# Get user information
name, age = get_name_and_age()   # Unpack the returned
tuple

# Display the information
print(f"Your name is {name} and you are {age} years
old.")
```

Preparation (Explanation):

1. The return Statement:

- The return statement ends the execution of a function and sends a value back to the code that called the function.

- This returned value can be a number, a string, a boolean, a list, a dictionary, or even another function!

- If a function doesn't have a return statement, it implicitly returns None.

2. **Examples:**

   - **square(number) Function:**

     - Takes a number as input.

     - Calculates the square of the number (number * number).

     - Returns the calculated result.

   - **get_name_and_age() Function:**

     - Asks the user for their name and age.

     - Returns both the name and age as a tuple. (Tuples are handy for returning multiple values.)

Final Dish (Output):

```
Enter a number: 6.5
The square of 6.5 is 42.25

Enter your name: Alice
Enter your age: 30
Your name is Alice and you are 30 years old.
```

Why is this important?

- **Outputting Results:** Functions are often used to perform calculations or manipulations on data. The return statement allows you to get the results of these operations back from the function so you can use them in your main program.

- **Modular Code:** Functions with return values promote modularity and code reusability. You can write functions to perform specific tasks and then use them like building blocks in your larger programs.

- **Information Exchange:** Functions can be used to collect information from the user or external sources and then return that information to the main program for further processing.

Recipe 44: Default Arguments and Variable-Length Arguments (*args, **kwargs)

Ingredients (Code):

```python
# Python
# Default arguments
def greet(name, greeting="Hello"):
    """Greets a person with a customizable message."""
    print(f"{greeting}, {name}!")

greet("Alice")              # Uses the default greeting: "Hello"
greet("Bob", "Howdy")       # Overrides the default with "Howdy"

# Variable-length arguments (*args)
def add(*numbers):
    """Adds any number of numeric arguments."""
    total = 0
    for num in numbers:
        total += num
    return total

print(add(2, 3))            # Output: 5
print(add(1, 4, 6))         # Output: 11

# Variable-length keyword arguments (**kwargs)
def build_profile(first, last, **user_info):
    """Builds a dictionary containing user information."""
    user_info['first_name'] = first
    user_info['last_name'] = last
    return user_info

profile = build_profile('Albert', 'Einstein',
location='Princeton', field='Physics')
print(profile)
```

Preparation (Explanation):

1. **Default Arguments:**

   - You can provide default values for function parameters.

   - If a caller doesn't supply a value for a parameter with a default value, the default is used.

126

- In greet(), greeting defaults to "Hello" unless overridden.

2. **Variable-Length Arguments (*args):**

- The *args parameter allows you to pass an arbitrary number of positional arguments to a function.

- Inside the function, args is a tuple containing all the passed values.

- In add(), numbers is a tuple containing all the numbers you pass.

3. **Variable-Length Keyword Arguments (**kwargs):**

- The **kwargs parameter allows you to pass an arbitrary number of keyword arguments (name-value pairs) to a function.

- Inside the function, kwargs is a dictionary containing all the passed keyword arguments.

- In build_profile(), user_info is a dictionary that captures additional information like 'location' and 'field'.

Final Dish (Output):

```
Hello, Alice!
Howdy, Bob!
5
11
{'location': 'Princeton', 'field': 'Physics',
'first_name': 'Albert', 'last_name': 'Einstein'}
```

Why is this important?

- **Flexibility:** Default arguments and variable-length arguments make your functions more flexible and able to handle a wider range of input scenarios.

- **Cleaner Code:** *args and **kwargs can help you avoid long parameter lists, especially when the number of arguments can vary.

- **Extensibility:** You can add new parameters to a function without breaking existing code that calls it (if the new parameters have default values).

Recipe 45: Recursive Functions

Ingredients (Code):

```python
# Python
# Factorial calculation using recursion
def factorial(n):
    """Calculates the factorial of a non-negative
integer n."""
    if n == 0:
        return 1  # Base case: 0! = 1
    else:
        return n * factorial(n - 1)   # Recursive step

# Calculate factorial of 5
number = 5
result = factorial(number)
print(f"The factorial of {number} is {result}")


# Fibonacci sequence using recursion
def fibonacci(n):
    """Calculates the nth Fibonacci number."""
    if n <= 1:
        return n  # Base cases: 0 and 1
    else:
        return fibonacci(n - 1) + fibonacci(n - 2)   #
Recursive step

# Get the 10th Fibonacci number
fib_number = 10
result = fibonacci(fib_number)
print(f"The {fib_number}th Fibonacci number is
{result}")
```

Preparation (Explanation):

1. What is Recursion?

- Recursion is a programming technique where a function solves a problem by calling itself with a smaller input.

- It involves breaking down a problem into smaller, identical subproblems until you reach a base case that can be solved directly.

2. Examples:

- **Factorial:**

  - The factorial(n) function calculates the factorial of a number (e.g., 5! = 5 * 4 * 3 * 2 * 1).

  - Base Case: If n is 0, it returns 1 (0! = 1 by definition).

  - Recursive Step: If n is not 0, it calculates n times the factorial of n - 1 (e.g., 5! = 5 * 4!). This calls the factorial function again with a smaller input (4), and so on, until it reaches the base case.

- **Fibonacci:**

  - The fibonacci(n) function calculates the nth Fibonacci number in the sequence (0, 1, 1, 2, 3, 5, 8, ...).

  - Base Cases: If n is 0 or 1, it returns n.

  - Recursive Step: If n is greater than 1, it calculates the sum of the two previous Fibonacci numbers (fibonacci(n-1) + fibonacci(n-2)).

Final Dish (Output):

```
The factorial of 5 is 120
The 10th Fibonacci number is 55
```

Why is this important?

- **Elegant Solutions:** Recursion can provide elegant and concise solutions to problems that have a recursive structure.

- **Mathematical Foundations:** Many mathematical concepts are naturally recursive (e.g., factorials, Fibonacci numbers, tree structures), and recursion can be a powerful way to implement these concepts in code.

Important Considerations:

- **Base Case:** Every recursive function must have a base case that stops the recursion, preventing infinite loops.

- **Performance:** Recursion can be computationally expensive for large inputs due to the overhead of repeated function calls. Sometimes, an iterative (loop-based) solution might be more efficient.

10. File I/O:

Recipe 46: Opening, Reading, and Writing Files

Ingredients (Code):

```python
# Python
# Writing to a file
filename = "output.txt"

with open(filename, "w") as file:
    file.write("This is the first line.\n")
    file.write("This is the second line.\n")

print(f"Wrote to file: {filename}")

# Reading from a file
with open(filename, "r") as file:
    contents = file.read()  # Read entire file

print("\nFile Contents:")
print(contents)

# Appending to a file
with open(filename, "a") as file:
    file.write("This is an appended line.\n")

print("Appended to file.")

# Read the updated file contents
with open(filename, "r") as file:
    updated_contents = file.read()

print("\nUpdated File Contents:")
print(updated_contents)
```

Preparation (Explanation):

1. **Opening a File (with open()):**

    - open(filename, mode) is used to open a file.

    - **filename:** The path to the file you want to open.

    - **mode:** Specifies how you want to interact with the file:

- **"w":** Write mode (creates a new file or overwrites an existing one).

- **"r":** Read mode (default).

- **"a":** Append mode (adds to the end of the file).

- **"r+":** Read and write mode.

- **with open()... as file::** This is a context manager that ensures the file is closed properly when you're done with it, even if an error occurs.

2. **Writing to a File (.write()):**

- **file.write(text):** Writes the given text to the file.

- The \n character adds a newline (line break).

3. **Reading from a File (.read()):**

- **file.read():** Reads the entire contents of the file and returns it as a single string.

4. **Appending to a File (.write() in append mode):**

- When opening the file in "a" (append) mode, file.write() adds new text to the end without overwriting existing content.

Final Dish (Output):

```
Wrote to file: output.txt

File Contents:
This is the first line.
This is the second line.

Appended to file.

Updated File Contents:
This is the first line.
This is the second line.
```

Why is this important?

- **Persistent Data:** Files allow you to save data permanently so it can be used later, even after your program ends.

- **Data Exchange:** Files are a common way to share data between different programs or systems.

- **Configuration and Logging:** Files are often used to store configuration settings and log information for applications.

Important Considerations:

- **File Paths:** Always provide the correct path to your file, either relative to your script's location or as an absolute path.

- **Error Handling:** Be prepared to handle situations where files might not exist, be inaccessible, or contain unexpected data.

Recipe 47: Working with Different File Modes (read, write, append)

Ingredients (Code):

```python
# Python
# Write mode ("w")
with open("data.txt", "w") as file:
    file.write("This will overwrite any existing
content.\n")
    file.write("Only this new data will be saved.\n")
print("Data written in write mode.")


# Read mode ("r")
with open("data.txt", "r") as file:
    contents = file.read()
    print("\nReading the file (after write):\n",
contents)


# Append mode ("a")
with open("data.txt", "a") as file:
    file.write("This is appended to the existing data.
\n")
print("Data appended to the file.")


# Read and Write mode ("r+")
with open("data.txt", "r+") as file:
    original_content = file.read() # Reading original
content
    file.seek(0) # Moving cursor to the beginning
    file.write("This is added at the beginning.\n")  #
Adding at the beginning
    file.write(original_content) # Adding the original
content back

print("\nReading the file (after read & write):")
with open("data.txt", "r") as file:
    final_contents = file.read()
    print(final_contents)
```

Preparation (Explanation):

1. Write Mode ("w"):

- Opens the file for writing.

- If the file exists, its contents are truncated (erased).

- If the file doesn't exist, a new file is created.

- Used to create new files or completely overwrite existing ones.

2. **Read Mode ("r"):**

   - Opens the file for reading only (default mode).

   - You can't modify the file's contents.

   - Used to access and process existing files.

3. **Append Mode ("a"):**

   - Opens the file for appending (adding to the end).

   - If the file doesn't exist, a new file is created.

   - Used to add data to existing files without overwriting them.

4. **Read and Write Mode ("r+"):**

   - Opens the file for both reading and writing.

   - The file pointer is placed at the beginning of the file.

   - Used to modify existing files.

   - file.seek(0) moves the file pointer to the beginning to enable reading the file content again.

Final Dish (Output):

```
Data written in write mode.

Reading the file (after write):
 This will overwrite any existing content.
 Only this new data will be saved.

Data appended to the file.

Reading the file (after read & write):
```

```
This is added at the beginning.
This will overwrite any existing content.
Only this new data will be saved.
This is appended to the existing data.
```

Why is this important?

- **File Handling:** Understanding different file modes is crucial for working with files effectively in Python. Choosing the correct mode ensures you interact with the file in the way you intend.

- **Data Persistence:** By writing data to files, you can store information persistently, making it available even after your program ends.

- **Data Manipulation:** You can use different modes to update existing data or add new information to files.

Recipe 48: File Paths and Directories

Ingredients (Code):

```python
# Python
import os
from pathlib import Path

# Get current working directory
cwd = os.getcwd()
print(f"Current working directory: {cwd}")

# Create a directory (if it doesn't exist)
directory = "my_data"
os.makedirs(directory, exist_ok=True)  # exist_ok=True
prevents error if already exists

# Construct file paths
file_path = os.path.join(directory, "data.txt")
print(f"Full file path: {file_path}")

# Pathlib for more object-oriented approach
p = Path(directory)
for file in p.iterdir():
    print(file)

# Check if path is a file or directory
if os.path.isfile(file_path):
    print(f"{file_path} is a file.")
else:
    print(f"{file_path} is not a file.")

if os.path.isdir(directory):
    print(f"{directory} is a directory.")

# Get file name and extension
file_name = os.path.basename(file_path)
base_name, extension = os.path.splitext(file_name)
print(f"File name: {file_name}, Base name: {base_name},
Extension: {extension}")
```

Preparation (Explanation):

1. **Import Modules:**

    - **os:** Provides functions for interacting with the operating system, including file and directory operations.

- **pathlib (Python 3.4+):** Offers an object-oriented way to work with paths, often making code more readable.

2. **Get Current Working Directory:**

   - **os.getcwd():** Returns the current working directory (the folder where your Python script is running) as a string.

3. **Create a Directory:**

   - **os.makedirs(directory, exist_ok=True):**

     - Creates the directory specified by directory if it doesn't already exist.

     - The exist_ok=True argument prevents an error if the directory is already present.

4. **Construct File Paths:**

   - **os.path.join(directory, "data.txt"):** Joins the directory name (directory) with a filename ("data.txt") using the correct separator for your operating system.

5. **Pathlib:**

   - Provides objects representing files and directories.

   - .iterdir() method allows you to iterate over files within a directory.

6. **Checking File/Directory Existence:**

   - **os.path.isfile(path):** Returns True if path points to a file.

- **os.path.isdir(path):** Returns True if path points to a directory.

7. **Getting File Name and Extension:**

   - **os.path.basename(path):** Returns the last component of a path (usually the file name).

   - **os.path.splitext(path):** Splits a path into its base name and file extension.

Final Dish (Output):

```
Current working directory: /Users/yourname/documents/
myproject
Full file path: my_data/data.txt
my_data/data.txt
my_data/.DS_Store
my_data/data.txt is a file.
my_data is a directory.
File name: data.txt, Base name: data, Extension: .txt
```

(The exact output for the p.iterdir() will vary depending on the files in your directory.)

Why is this important?

- **File Access:** Understanding file paths is crucial for reading and writing data to files.

- **Directory Management:** You'll often need to create, navigate, and manipulate directories to organize your project files.

- **Cross-Platform Compatibility:** Python's os module and pathlib make it easier to write code that works across different operating systems (Windows, macOS, Linux).

Recipe 49: Reading and Writing CSV Files

Ingredients (Code):

```python
# Python
import csv

# Data to write to the CSV file
data = [
    ["Name", "Age", "City"],
    ["Alice", "30", "New York"],
    ["Bob", "25", "London"],
    ["Charlie", "35", "Tokyo"]
]

# Writing to a CSV file
with open("people.csv", "w", newline="") as csvfile:
    writer = csv.writer(csvfile)
    writer.writerows(data)  # Write all rows at once
    print(f"Wrote data to people.csv")


# Reading from a CSV file
with open("people.csv", "r") as csvfile:
    reader = csv.reader(csvfile)
    for row in reader:
        print(row)  # Print each row as a list
```

Preparation (Explanation):

1. **Import the csv Module:** This line imports the csv module, which provides tools for working with CSV (Comma-Separated Values) files.

2. **Data Structure (List of Lists):**

   - The data variable is a list of lists, where each inner list represents a row in the CSV file.

   - The first row is typically used for column headers.

3. **Writing to a CSV File:**

   - **with open("people.csv", "w", newline="") as csvfile:** Opens the file people.csv in write mode ("w"). The newline="" argument is important to avoid extra blank lines on Windows.

141

- **writer = csv.writer(csvfile):** Creates a csv.writer object to handle writing to the file.

- **writer.writerows(data):** Writes all the rows from the data list into the CSV file.

4. **Reading from a CSV File:**

   - **with open("people.csv", "r") as csvfile:** Opens the file in read mode ("r").

   - **reader = csv.reader(csvfile):** Creates a csv.reader object to read data from the file.

   - **for row in reader:** Iterates over each row in the CSV file.

   - **print(row):** Prints each row, which is represented as a list of strings (one string per cell).

Final Dish (Output):

```
Wrote data to people.csv
['Name', 'Age', 'City']
['Alice', '30', 'New York']
['Bob', '25', 'London']
['Charlie', '35', 'Tokyo']
```

Why is this important?

- **Data Exchange:** CSV is a very common and simple format for storing and exchanging tabular data (data in rows and columns).

- **Data Analysis:** CSV files are frequently used as input for data analysis and manipulation libraries like Pandas.

- **Human Readable:** While simple, CSV files can be easily viewed and edited in text editors or spreadsheet programs like Excel.

Additional Notes:

- **Customization:** You can customize the delimiter (the character separating values in a row), quote character, and other aspects of the CSV format using the csv module's options.

- **Dictionary Reader/Writer:** The csv module also provides csv.DictReader and csv.DictWriter for reading and writing CSV data as dictionaries, where keys are the column names.

- **Large Files:** For very large CSV files, consider using techniques like reading the file in chunks to avoid memory issues.

Recipe 50: JSON Serialization and Deserialization

Ingredients (Code):

```python
# Python
import json

# Data to be serialized (Python objects)
data = {
    "name": "Alice",
    "age": 30,
    "city": "New York",
    "has_pets": True,
    "hobbies": ["coding", "music", "hiking"]
}

# Serialization (Python objects to JSON string)
json_string = json.dumps(data, indent=4)  # indent for
pretty-printing

print("JSON String:")
print(json_string)

# Save JSON string to a file
with open("data.json", "w") as jsonfile:
    json.dump(data, jsonfile, indent=4)
print("Data saved to data.json")


# Deserialization (JSON string to Python objects)
data_from_string = json.loads(json_string)
print("\nData from JSON String:")
print(data_from_string)

# Load JSON data from a file
with open("data.json", "r") as jsonfile:
    data_from_file = json.load(jsonfile)
print("\nData from JSON File:")
print(data_from_file)
```

Preparation (Explanation):

1. **Import the json Module:**

    - This module provides functions for working with
      JSON (JavaScript Object Notation) data, a popular
      format for storing and exchanging information.

2. **Data Structure:**

144

- The data variable is a Python dictionary, which is a natural fit for JSON since JSON objects are essentially key-value pairs.

- Note how the dictionary can hold different data types: strings, integers, booleans, and lists.

3. **Serialization (json.dumps and json.dump):**

   - json.dumps(data, indent=4):

     - Converts the Python dictionary (data) into a JSON-formatted string.

     - indent=4 adds indentation for better readability (optional).

   - json.dump(data, jsonfile, indent=4):

     - Writes the Python data directly to a file in JSON format.

4. **Deserialization (json.loads and json.load):**

   - **json.loads(json_string):**

     - Parses a JSON string and converts it back into a Python dictionary.

   - **json.load(jsonfile):**

     - Reads JSON data from a file and returns it as corresponding Python objects.

Final Dish (Output):

```
JSON String:
{
    "name": "Alice",
    "age": 30,
    "city": "New York",
    "has_pets": true,
    "hobbies": [
```

```
            "coding",
            "music",
            "hiking"
      ]
}
Data saved to data.json

Data from JSON String:
{'name': 'Alice', 'age': 30, 'city': 'New York',
'has_pets': True, 'hobbies': ['coding', 'music',
'hiking']}

Data from JSON File:
{'name': 'Alice', 'age': 30, 'city': 'New York',
'has_pets': True, 'hobbies': ['coding', 'music',
'hiking']}
```

Why is this important?

- **Data Interchange:** JSON is a widely used format for exchanging data between different systems and programming languages.

- **Web APIs:** Most web APIs use JSON to send and receive data.

- **Configuration Files:** JSON is often used for storing configuration settings in a human-readable format.

- **Data Persistence:** You can save data in JSON format to files for later use.

11. Modules:

Recipe 51: Importing Modules and Using Functions

Ingredients (Code):

```python
# Python
# Importing modules
import math
import random

# Using functions from the math module
number = 16
sqrt_result = math.sqrt(number)  # Calculate square root
print(f"The square root of {number} is {sqrt_result}")

angle_degrees = 45
angle_radians = math.radians(angle_degrees)  # Convert
degrees to radians
sin_result = math.sin(angle_radians)          # Calculate
sine
print(f"The sine of {angle_degrees} degrees is
{sin_result:.4f}")  # Format to 4 decimals

# Using functions from the random module
random_int = random.randint(1, 100)  # Random integer
between 1 and 100 (inclusive)
print(f"Random integer: {random_int}")

items = ["apple", "banana", "orange"]
random_choice = random.choice(items)  # Choose a random
item from the list
print(f"Random choice: {random_choice}")
```

Preparation (Explanation):

1. **Importing Modules:**

   - **import math:** Imports the entire math module, which provides mathematical functions and constants.

   - **import random:** Imports the random module, which offers functions for generating random numbers and making random choices.

2. **Using Functions:**

- **math.sqrt(number):** Calls the sqrt() function from the math module to calculate the square root of the number variable.

- **math.radians(angle_degrees):** Converts the angle_degrees value from degrees to radians.

- **math.sin(angle_radians):** Calculates the sine of the angle in radians.

- **random.randint(1, 100):** Generates a random integer between 1 and 100 (inclusive).

- **random.choice(items):** Selects a random item from the items list.

3. **Dot Notation:**

- To access functions or attributes within a module, use the dot (.) notation: module_name.function_name or module_name.attribute_name.

- For example, math.sqrt refers to the sqrt function within the math module.

Final Dish (Output):

```
The square root of 16 is 4.0
The sine of 45 degrees is 0.7071
Random integer: 57   (Your result will vary)
Random choice: banana   (Your result will vary)
```

Why is this important?

- **Code Reusability:** Modules allow you to reuse code that others have already written, saving you time and effort. Python's standard library is rich with modules for various tasks.

- **Organization:** Modules help organize code into logical units, making your projects easier to manage and understand.

- **Namespace Management:** Modules create separate namespaces, preventing naming conflicts between your code and the module's code.

Additional Ways to Import:

```Python
from math import sqrt, sin, radians  # Import specific
functions
from random import *                 # Import everything
from the random module (use with caution!)
```

Key Points:

- **Choose the right module:** Python has a vast collection of modules. Refer to the Python documentation to find the right module for your needs.

- **Organize imports:** It's good practice to group your import statements at the beginning of your file.

Recipe 52: Creating Your Own Modules

Ingredients (Code):

File: my_module.py

```python
# Python
def greet(name):
    """Greets the person with the given name."""
    return f"Hello, {name}!"

def square(x):
    """Calculates the square of a number."""
    return x * x
```

File: main.py

```python
# Python
# Importing the module
import my_module

# Using functions from the module
message = my_module.greet("Alice")
print(message)

result = my_module.square(5)
print(f"The square of 5 is: {result}")
```

Preparation (Explanation):

1. **Creating a Module:**

    - A module is simply a Python file (e.g., my_module.py) that contains functions, classes, or variables you want to reuse in other parts of your project.

    - In this example, my_module.py defines two functions: greet(name) and square(x).

2. **Importing the Module:**

    - In your main script (main.py), use the import statement to load the module.

    - import my_module makes the functions and variables within my_module.py available for use.

3. Using Functions from the Module:

- Use dot notation (module_name.function_name) to access and call functions from the imported module.

- my_module.greet("Alice") calls the greet function from my_module and passes the string "Alice" as an argument.

- my_module.square(5) calls the square function with the argument 5.

Final Dish (Output):

```
Hello, Alice!
The square of 5 is: 25
```

Why is this important?

- **Code Organization:** Modules help you organize your code into manageable chunks. Related functions and classes can be grouped together in a single file, making your project more structured.

- **Code Reusability:** By putting your code in modules, you can easily reuse it in different parts of your project or even in other projects.

- **Maintainability:** Modules make your code more maintainable because you can update a module without having to change every script that uses it.

Key Points:

- **File Names:** Module filenames should have the .py extension.

- **Naming Conventions:** Use lowercase letters and underscores for module names (e.g., my_utils, data_processing).

151

- **Avoid Name Collisions:** Be mindful of naming conflicts. If two modules you import have functions with the same name, you can use aliases to avoid confusion (e.g., import pandas as pd).

- **__name__ Variable:** Each module has a special variable called __name__. When a module is run directly as a script, its __name__ is set to "__main__". You can use this to include code that should run only when the module is executed as the main program (see Recipe 34 for an example).

Recipe 53: Understanding __name__ == "__main__"

Ingredients (Code):

File: my_functions.py

```python
# Python
def say_hello(name):
    """Greets the person with the given name."""
    return f"Hello, {name}!"

def main():
    """Example function to be run as a script."""
    print(say_hello("World"))

# This block executes ONLY if the file is run as a
script
if __name__ == "__main__":
    main()
```

Preparation (Explanation):

1. **The __name__ Variable:**

   - Every Python module has a special built-in variable named __name__.

   - When a module is imported, its __name__ is set to the name of the module (e.g., "my_functions").

   - However, when a Python file is run as a script (from the command line or by executing it directly), its __name__ is set to the special string "__main__".

2. **The if __name__ == "__main__": Block:**

   - This conditional block is used to check whether the current file is being run as the main program or being imported as a module.

- If the file is run as a script: The condition __name__ == "__main__" is True, and the code inside the block is executed.

- If the file is imported: The condition is False, and the code inside the block is skipped.

3. **Why Use It?**

- Testing and Debugging: You can place code for testing your module's functions inside this block. When you run the module as a script, your tests will execute, but they won't run when the module is imported elsewhere.

- Running as a Script or Module: This allows you to design your module to be both a reusable library of functions and a standalone script with a specific entry point (the main() function in this example).

Final Dish (Output):

Running as a script (e.g., python my_functions.py):

```
Hello, World!
```

Importing as a module (in another Python file):

```
Python
import my_functions

message = my_functions.say_hello("Alice")
print(message)   # Output: Hello, Alice!
```

In this case, only the say_hello() function is available for use; the code inside the if __name__ == "__main__": block is not executed.

Recipe 54: Exploring the Standard Library (os, sys, datetime, math)

Ingredients (Code):

```python
# Python
import os
import sys
import datetime
import math

# os module: Operating system interactions
print("Operating System:", os.name)          # Get the
operating system name
print("Current Directory:", os.getcwd())    # Get current
working directory
print("Environment Variables:", os.environ)  # Access
environment variables

# sys module: System-specific parameters and functions
print("Python Version:", sys.version)
print("Command Line Arguments:", sys.argv) # Get
command-line arguments as a list

# datetime module: Date and time manipulation
now = datetime.datetime.now()
print("Current Date and Time:", now)
formatted_time = now.strftime("%Y-%m-%d %H:%M:%S")
print("Formatted Time:", formatted_time)

# math module: Mathematical functions
pi_value = math.pi
print("Pi:", pi_value)
factorial_5 = math.factorial(5)
print("5! (Factorial of 5):", factorial_5)
```

Preparation (Explanation):

1. **os Module:**

   - **os.name:** Returns the name of the operating system (e.g., 'posix' for macOS/Linux, 'nt' for Windows).

   - **os.getcwd():** Gets the current working directory (the folder your script is running from).

- **os.environ:** A dictionary-like object containing environment variables.

2. **sys Module:**

   - **sys.version:** Provides information about the Python version you're using.

   - **sys.argv:** A list of command-line arguments passed to your script. The first element (sys.argv[0]) is usually the script name itself.

3. **datetime Module:**

   - **datetime.datetime.now():** Gets the current date and time.

   - **strftime("%Y-%m-%d %H:%M:%S"):** Formats the date and time into a string using directives like %Y (year), %m (month), %d (day), %H (hour), %M (minute), and %S (second).

4. **math Module:**

   - **math.pi:** The mathematical constant pi.

   - **math.factorial(n):** Calculates the factorial of a number n (n! = 1 * 2 * 3 * ... * n).

Final Dish (Output):

```
Operating System: posix  (or nt for Windows)
Current Directory: /path/to/your/project
Environment Variables: environ({'USER': 'yourname',
'HOME': '/Users/yourname', ...}) # Your environment
variables
Python Version: 3.x.x (Your Python version)
Command Line Arguments: ['/path/to/your/script.py']

Current Date and Time: 2024-06-12 16:54:24.920296
Formatted Time: 2024-06-12 16:54:24
Pi: 3.141592653589793
5! (Factorial of 5): 120
```

Why is this important?

- **System Interaction:** The os and sys modules enable your Python scripts to interact with the underlying operating system, get information about the environment, and handle command-line arguments.

- **Time Operations:** The datetime module is essential for working with dates, times, and time intervals. It's used in applications like scheduling, logging, data analysis, and financial calculations.

- **Math Functions:** The math module provides a wide range of mathematical functions for trigonometry, logarithms, exponentials, and other calculations.

Recipe 55: Installing Third-Party Modules (pip)

Ingredients (Terminal Commands):

```bash
# Bash
# Install a specific module (e.g., NumPy)
pip install numpy

# Install multiple modules
pip install requests beautifulsoup4

# Install a specific version
pip install pandas==1.5.3

# Upgrade an existing module
pip install --upgrade numpy

# Uninstall a module
pip uninstall numpy
```

Preparation (Explanation):

1. **What is pip?**

   - pip is the package installer for Python. It's a command-line tool that comes pre-installed with most Python distributions (Python 2.7.9+ and Python 3.4+).

   - It allows you to easily download and install packages (modules) from the Python Package Index (PyPI) – the official repository for third-party Python software.

2. **Basic pip Commands:**

   - **pip install <module_name>:** Downloads and installs the specified module and its dependencies.

   - **pip install <module1> <module2> ...:** Installs multiple modules at once.

- **pip install <module_name>==<version>:** Installs a specific version of a module.

- **pip install --upgrade <module_name>:** Upgrades an existing module to the latest version.

- **pip uninstall <module_name>:** Removes a module.

3. **Virtual Environments (Recommended):**

   - Before installing modules, consider creating a virtual environment. This isolates the packages for a specific project, preventing conflicts with other projects or your system-wide Python installation.

   - To create a virtual environment (using the built-in venv module):

```bash
# Bash
python -m venv my_project_env
```

   - Activate the environment before using pip:

```bash
# Bash
# On Windows:
my_project_env\Scripts\activate

# On macOS/Linux:
source my_project_env/bin/activate
```

Final Dish (No Direct Output):

- Installing modules doesn't produce output in your Python scripts. Instead, it modifies your Python environment by adding the new packages.

- You can verify the installation by trying to import the module in your code:

```
# Python
import numpy  # If no errors, NumPy is
successfully installed
```

Why is this important?

- **Extending Functionality:** Third-party modules greatly expand Python's capabilities. They offer specialized tools and libraries for tasks like data analysis (NumPy, Pandas), web development (Flask, Django), machine learning (scikit-learn), and much more.

- **Community Contributions:** PyPI hosts thousands of open-source modules contributed by the Python community, allowing you to leverage solutions created by others.

- **Keeping Up-to-Date:** Regularly upgrading modules ensures you have access to the latest features, bug fixes, and security patches.

Important Considerations:

- **Check for Compatibility:** Ensure that the modules you install are compatible with your Python version.

- **Dependency Management:** pip automatically handles installing any dependencies required by the modules you install.

- **Virtual Environments:** Using virtual environments (like venv) is highly recommended to keep your projects organized and avoid dependency conflicts.

12. Error Handling:

Recipe 56: Try-Except Blocks (Catching Exceptions)

Ingredients (Code):

```python
# Python
def divide(x, y):
    """Divides x by y, handling potential
ZeroDivisionError."""
    try:
        result = x / y
        print(f"The result of {x} / {y} is: {result}")
    except ZeroDivisionError:
        print("Error: Division by zero is not allowed.")
    except TypeError as e:
        print(f"Error: Invalid input types. {e}")

# Examples
divide(10, 2)       # Valid division
divide(5, 0)        # ZeroDivisionError
divide("10", 5)     # TypeError
```

Preparation (Explanation):

1. **Try-Except Structure:**

   - **try:** This block contains the code you suspect might raise an exception. In our case, the division operation x / y could potentially lead to a ZeroDivisionError.

   - **except ExceptionType:** These blocks handle specific types of exceptions.

     - The first except block catches ZeroDivisionError and prints a custom error message.

     - The second except block catches TypeError (if the input types are not numbers) and prints a more specific message along with the error details obtained through as e.

2. **How It Works:**

- The code inside the try block is executed.

- If no exception occurs, the code continues after the try-except structure.

- If an exception of the specified type occurs (e.g., ZeroDivisionError or TypeError), the corresponding except block is executed.

- If the exception doesn't match any of the except blocks, it will propagate up and potentially crash your program.

Final Dish (Output):

```
The result of 10 / 2 is: 5.0
Error: Division by zero is not allowed.
Error: Invalid input types. unsupported operand type(s)
for /: 'str' and 'int'
```

Why is this important?

- **Graceful Error Handling:** try-except blocks prevent your program from crashing unexpectedly when it encounters errors (exceptions).

- **User-Friendly Messages:** You can provide informative error messages to the user, helping them understand what went wrong.

- **Robustness:** By handling exceptions, you make your code more robust and able to recover from unexpected situations.

Key Points:

- **Multiple Except Blocks:** You can have multiple except blocks to handle different types of exceptions.

- **Catch-All (except Exception):** You can have a general except block (without specifying an exception type) to catch any unexpected error. However, this is less informative and should be used sparingly.

- **finally Block:** An optional finally block can be added after the except blocks. Code in the finally block always executes, whether an exception occurred or not, making it suitable for cleanup tasks (e.g., closing files).

Recipe 57: Raising Exceptions

Ingredients (Code):

```python
# Python
def calculate_age(year_born):
    """Calculates a person's age, raising exceptions for
invalid input."""

    current_year = 2024

    if not isinstance(year_born, int):
        raise TypeError("Input year must be an
integer.")
    if year_born > current_year:
        raise ValueError("Year of birth cannot be in the
future.")
    if year_born < 1900: # Adjust the minimum year for
your use case
        raise ValueError("Year of birth seems
unlikely.")

    age = current_year - year_born
    return age

# Example usage
try:
    age = calculate_age(1990)
    print(f"You are {age} years old.")

    age = calculate_age(2030) # Try entering a year in
the future
    print(f"You are {age} years old.")

    age = calculate_age("hello") # Try entering a non-
integer value
    print(f"You are {age} years old.")
except ValueError as e:
    print(e)   # Print the ValueError message
except TypeError as e:
    print(e)   # Print the TypeError message
```

Preparation (Explanation):

1. The raise Statement:

- The raise statement is used to explicitly trigger an exception.

- You can raise built-in exceptions or create your own custom exceptions (covered in a later recipe).

- raise ExceptionType("Error message"): Creates and raises an exception of the specified type with a descriptive error message.

2. **Example Function calculate_age():**

   - This function calculates a person's age based on their year of birth.

   - It includes input validation:

     - **if not isinstance(year_born, int):** Checks if year_born is an integer. If not, it raises a TypeError.

     - **if year_born > current_year:** Checks if year_born is in the future. If so, it raises a ValueError.

     - **if year_born < 1900:** An arbitrary example check. Here, you would define your own limits. If outside them, it raises a ValueError.

3. **Handling Exceptions:**

   - The try-except block is used to catch and handle the exceptions raised by calculate_age().

   - The except blocks print the error messages provided with the raised exceptions.

Final Dish (Output):

```
You are 34 years old.
Year of birth cannot be in the future.
Input year must be an integer.
```

Why is this important?

- **Input Validation:** Raising exceptions is a powerful way to validate input and ensure your functions receive valid data.

- **Error Signaling:** Exceptions provide a clear way to signal that something has gone wrong in your code.

- **Custom Errors:** You can define your own exception types to handle specific errors in your application logic.

Recipe 58: Exception Types (ValueError, TypeError, ZeroDivisionError, etc.)

Ingredients (Code):

```python
# Python
# ValueError: Raised when an operation receives an
argument of the correct type but an inappropriate value
try:
    int("abc")   # Trying to convert a non-numeric
string to an integer
except ValueError as e:
    print(f"ValueError: {e}")


# TypeError: Raised when an operation or function is
applied to an object of inappropriate type
try:
    "hello" + 5  # Trying to add a string and an integer
except TypeError as e:
    print(f"TypeError: {e}")

# ZeroDivisionError: Raised when the second argument of
a division or modulo operation is zero
try:
    10 / 0
except ZeroDivisionError as e:
    print(f"ZeroDivisionError: {e}")

# IndexError: Raised when trying to access an item at an
invalid index in a sequence (e.g., list, tuple, string)
my_list = [1, 2, 3]
try:
    print(my_list[5])   # Trying to access the 6th
element (index 5) of a 3-element list
except IndexError as e:
    print(f"IndexError: {e}")

# KeyError: Raised when a dictionary key is not found
my_dict = {"name": "Alice", "age": 30}
try:
    print(my_dict["city"])   # Trying to access a non-
existent key
except KeyError as e:
    print(f"KeyError: {e}")
```

Preparation (Explanation):

1. Built-in Exceptions:

- Python has many built-in exceptions to handle various types of errors that can occur during program execution.

- Each exception type has a specific meaning and purpose.

2. **Examples:**

- **ValueError:** Raised when you pass a value of the correct type but an inappropriate value to a function (e.g., trying to convert "abc" to an integer).

- **TypeError:** Raised when you try to perform an operation on an object that doesn't support it (e.g., adding a string and an integer).

- **ZeroDivisionError:** Raised when you attempt to divide by zero.

- **IndexError:** Raised when you try to access an index in a sequence that doesn't exist.

- **KeyError:** Raised when you try to access a key that's not in a dictionary.

Final Dish (Output):

```
ValueError: invalid literal for int() with base 10:
'abc'
TypeError: can only concatenate str (not "int") to str
ZeroDivisionError: division by zero
IndexError: list index out of range
KeyError: 'city'
```

Why is this important?

- **Error Handling:** Understanding the different types of exceptions is crucial for writing robust code that can handle errors gracefully.

- **Debugging:** Knowing which exceptions are raised for specific errors helps you pinpoint issues in your code.

- **Specific Handling:** You can use try-except blocks to catch and handle different exception types separately, tailoring your error responses accordingly.

Key Points:

- **Check the Python Documentation:** The Python documentation provides a comprehensive list of built-in exceptions (https://docs.python.org/3/library/exceptions.html).

- **Exception Hierarchy:** Exceptions are organized in a hierarchy, with more general exceptions like Exception at the top and more specific exceptions like ZeroDivisionError as subclasses.

Recipe 59: Custom Exceptions

Ingredients (Code):

```python
# Python
# Define a custom exception class
class InvalidAgeError(ValueError):
    """Raised when an input age is invalid."""
    pass  # The pass statement does nothing; it's a
placeholder

class NegativeBalanceError(Exception):
    """Raised when a bank account goes into negative
balance."""
    def __init__(self, message, deficit):
        super().__init__(message)
        self.deficit = deficit

# Function that uses the custom exception
def withdraw(balance, amount):
    """Withdraws money from a bank account."""
    if amount > balance:
        raise NegativeBalanceError("Insufficient funds",
amount - balance)
    else:
        return balance - amount

# Example usage
try:
    balance = 1000
    print(f"Initial balance: ${balance}")

    balance = withdraw(balance, 200)
    print(f"Balance after withdrawal: ${balance}")

    balance = withdraw(balance, 1000)
    print(f"Balance after withdrawal: ${balance}")
except NegativeBalanceError as e:
    print(f"Error: {e}. You are ${e.deficit} short.")
except InvalidAgeError as e:
    print(f"Error: {e}")
```

Preparation (Explanation):

1. Defining Custom Exceptions:

- Custom exceptions are created by subclassing the built-in Exception class (or one of its subclasses, like ValueError).

- **InvalidAgeError(ValueError):** This defines a custom exception named InvalidAgeError that inherits from ValueError. It's a good practice to make your custom exceptions specific so they convey meaningful information about the type of error.

2. **NegativeBalanceError with Attributes:**

   - This custom exception demonstrates how to add additional attributes (e.g., deficit) to provide more context about the error.

   - The __init__ method initializes the exception object and sets the deficit attribute.

3. **Raising Custom Exceptions:**

   - In the withdraw function, the raise statement is used to trigger the NegativeBalanceError when the withdrawal amount exceeds the balance.

   - Notice how we pass a message and the deficit amount to the exception.

4. **Handling Custom Exceptions:**

   - In the try-except block, we catch both NegativeBalanceError and InvalidAgeError.

   - The except blocks print custom error messages, including the deficit amount (if applicable) for NegativeBalanceError.

Final Dish (Output):

```
Initial balance: $1000
Balance after withdrawal: $800
Error: Insufficient funds. You are $200 short.
```

Why is this important?

- **Specific Error Handling:** Custom exceptions allow you to define errors that are specific to your application's logic, making your code more self-explanatory and easier to maintain.

- **Improved Readability:** Instead of using generic exceptions, you can use custom exception names that clearly convey the nature of the error.

- **Additional Information:** You can attach custom attributes to your exceptions to provide more context and details about the error.

Recipe 60: Finally Block (Cleanup Code)

Ingredients (Code):

```python
# Python
def process_file(filename):
    """Opens a file, processes its contents, and ensures
it's closed."""
    try:
        with open(filename, "r") as file:  # Use context
manager for automatic closing
            data = file.read()
            # Process data here (e.g., modify, analyze,
etc.)
            print(f"Processing data from: {filename}")

    except FileNotFoundError:
        print(f"Error: File '{filename}' not found.")

    finally:
        print(f"Closing file: {filename}")  # Always
executed


# Example usage
process_file("data.txt")    # Existing file
process_file("missing.txt")  # Non-existent file
```

Preparation (Explanation):

1. **The finally Block:**

   - **finally:** This optional block is placed after try and
     any except blocks.

   - **Guaranteed Execution:** The code
     inside finally is always executed, regardless of
     whether an exception was raised or not.

   - **Cleanup Tasks:** The finally block is primarily
     used for cleanup activities that must happen
     regardless of how the try block completes.

2. **Example Function (process_file):**

- **This function demonstrates a typical use case for finally:** ensuring a file is closed after it's opened.

- **The with open(filename, "r") as file:** statement is a context manager that automatically closes the file object when the block ends, even if an exception occurs.

- The finally block acts as an extra layer of safety, explicitly printing a message to confirm the file is being closed.

- In real-world scenarios, you would perform more complex cleanup tasks here, such as releasing resources, closing network connections, etc.

3. **Error Handling:**

- The except FileNotFoundError block catches a specific exception that could be raised if the file does not exist.

Final Dish (Output):

```
Processing data from: data.txt
Closing file: data.txt
Error: File 'missing.txt' not found.
Closing file: missing.txt
```

Why is this important?

- **Resource Management:** In programming, it's crucial to properly manage resources like files, network connections, and database handles. The finally block provides a reliable way to release these resources, preventing leaks and ensuring your program behaves correctly even when errors occur.

- **Robust Code:** By using finally for cleanup tasks, you make your code more robust and less prone to unexpected issues caused by unclosed resources.

- **Code Structure:** The finally block helps organize your code by separating error handling logic from the essential cleanup actions.

Additional Notes:

- In most cases, you'll want to use a context manager (like with open()) to handle file closing automatically. The finally block is an extra safeguard in case something goes wrong with the context manager itself.

- You can have a try block with only a finally block (no except blocks) if you don't need to handle specific exceptions but still want to ensure cleanup.

13. Object-Oriented Programming (OOP):

Recipe 61: Classes and Objects

Ingredients (Code):

```python
# Python
# Define a class
class Dog:
    """A simple class to represent a dog."""
    def __init__(self, name, breed, age):  # Constructor
        """Initializes the dog's attributes."""
        self.name = name
        self.breed = breed
        self.age = age

    def bark(self):  # Method
        """Simulates the dog barking."""
        print(f"{self.name} says Woof!")


# Create instances (objects) of the Dog class
dog1 = Dog("Buddy", "Golden Retriever", 3)
dog2 = Dog("Lucy", "Poodle", 5)

# Accessing attributes
print(f"{dog1.name} is a {dog1.breed} and is {dog1.age} years old.")
print(f"{dog2.name} is a {dog2.breed} and is {dog2.age} years old.")

# Calling methods
dog1.bark()
dog2.bark()
```

Preparation (Explanation):

1. **Class Definition (class Dog:):**

    - **Class:** A blueprint for creating objects (a particular data structure), providing initial values for state (member variables or attributes), and implementations of behavior (member functions or methods).

- **Dog:** The name of the class. We use PascalCase (capitalized words) for class names by convention.

- **Docstring:** Describes the purpose of the class.

2. **Constructor (__init__)**

   - **__init__(self, name, breed, age):**

     - This is a special method called the constructor. It's automatically called when you create a new instance of the class.

     - The self parameter refers to the instance of the object being created.

     - name, breed, and age are additional parameters for setting the initial attributes (properties) of the dog.

     - The constructor assigns the values passed as arguments to the self.name, self.breed, and self.age attributes of the object.

3. **Method (bark)**

   - **bark(self):**

     - This is a regular method (function) defined within the class.

     - The self parameter is required for all instance methods. It provides a way for the method to access the object's attributes.

     - This method simulates the dog barking.

4. **Creating Objects:**

   - **dog1 = Dog("Buddy", "Golden Retriever", 3)**

- This line creates an instance (object) of the Dog class named dog1.

- The arguments "Buddy", "Golden Retriever", and 3 are passed to the constructor to set the initial values of the name, breed, and age attributes.

- **dog2 = Dog("Lucy", "Poodle", 5)**

  - This creates another Dog object named dog2.

5. **Accessing Attributes and Calling Methods:**

   - **dog1.name, dog1.breed, dog1.age:** Accesses the attributes of the dog1 object.

   - **dog1.bark():** Calls the bark() method on the dog1 object.

Final Dish (Output):

```
Buddy is a Golden Retriever and is 3 years old.
Lucy is a Poodle and is 5 years old.
Buddy says Woof!
Lucy says Woof!
```

Why is this important?

- **Object-Oriented Programming (OOP):** Classes and objects are the foundation of OOP, a powerful programming paradigm that helps you model real-world entities and their interactions in your code.

- **Data Encapsulation:** Classes allow you to bundle data (attributes) and the functions that operate on that data (methods) together.

- **Modularity and Reusability:** You can create multiple objects from a single class, each with its own set of data.

This promotes code reusability and makes your code easier to maintain.

Recipe 62: Constructors and Destructors (__init__, __del__)

Ingredients (Code):

```python
# Python
class Book:
    """Represents a book object."""

    def __init__(self, title, author):
        """Constructor: Initializes a new book with
title and author."""
        self.title = title
        self.author = author
        print(f"A new book '{self.title}' by
{self.author} has been created.")

    def __del__(self):
        """Destructor: Called when the object is about
to be destroyed."""
        print(f"The book '{self.title}' is being
destroyed. Goodbye!")

# Create book objects
book1 = Book("The Hitchhiker's Guide to the Galaxy",
"Douglas Adams")
book2 = Book("Pride and Prejudice", "Jane Austen")

# The rest of your program...

# When the program ends (or when these objects go out of
scope)
del book1
del book2  # Explicitly call destructor for
demonstration (not always necessary)
```

Preparation (Explanation):

1. **Constructor (__init__)**

   - **Purpose:** The constructor is a special method that is automatically called when you create a new object (instance) of the class.

   - **Initialization:** It's used to initialize the object's attributes (its data or properties) with appropriate values.

- **__init__(self, title, author):**

  - **self:** A reference to the object being created.

  - **title, author:** Arguments you provide when creating the object.

  - Inside the constructor, we assign these values to the self.title and self.author attributes.

2. **Destructor (__del__)**

   - **Purpose:** The destructor is another special method that is called when an object is about to be destroyed by the garbage collector (when there are no more references to the object).

   - **Clean-up:** It's used for any necessary cleanup actions, such as closing files, releasing resources, or logging messages.

   - **__del__(self):**

     - **self:** A reference to the object being destroyed.

     - In this example, the destructor simply prints a message indicating the book is being destroyed.

Final Dish (Output):

```
A new book 'The Hitchhiker's Guide to the Galaxy' by
Douglas Adams has been created.
A new book 'Pride and Prejudice' by Jane Austen has been
created.
# ... (rest of your program output)
The book 'The Hitchhiker's Guide to the Galaxy' is being
destroyed. Goodbye!
The book 'Pride and Prejudice' is being destroyed.
Goodbye!
```

Why is this important?

- **Object Initialization:** Constructors ensure that objects are created in a valid state with the necessary initial values.

- **Resource Management:** Destructors help you gracefully release resources (like open files or network connections) when objects are no longer needed, preventing leaks and ensuring proper cleanup.

- **OOP Best Practices:** Using constructors and destructors (when necessary) promotes well-organized and maintainable object-oriented code.

Important Considerations:

- **Garbage Collection:** Python's garbage collector usually handles object destruction automatically, so you don't always need to explicitly define destructors.

- **Deterministic Cleanup:** If you need to ensure that resources are released at a specific time (not just when the garbage collector runs), consider using context managers (with the with statement) instead of destructors.

Recipe 63: Instance Variables and Methods

Ingredients (Code):

```python
# Python
class Car:
    """Represents a car object."""

    def __init__(self, make, model, year):
        """Initializes the car's attributes."""
        self.make = make  # Instance variable for make
        self.model = model  # Instance variable for
model
        self.year = year  # Instance variable for year
        self.odometer_reading = 0  # Instance variable
for odometer (initialized to 0)

    def get_descriptive_name(self):
        """Returns a formatted description of the
car."""
        long_name = f"{self.year} {self.make}
{self.model}"
        return long_name.title()

    def read_odometer(self):
        """Prints the current odometer reading."""
        print(f"This car has {self.odometer_reading}
miles on it.")

    def update_odometer(self, mileage):
        """
        Sets the odometer reading to the given value.
        Rejects the change if it attempts to roll the
odometer back.
        """
        if mileage >= self.odometer_reading:
            self.odometer_reading = mileage
        else:
            print("You can't roll back an odometer!")

# Create a car object
my_car = Car("Toyota", "Camry", 2023)

# Print its description
print(my_car.get_descriptive_name())  # Call the
instance method

# Read initial odometer reading
my_car.read_odometer()

# Update the odometer
```

```
my_car.update_odometer(23500)
my_car.read_odometer()
```

Preparation (Explanation):

1. Instance Variables:

- Instance variables are specific to each instance (object) of a class.

- They store data that is unique to each object.

- In this example, make, model, year, and odometer_reading are instance variables.

- They are defined within the constructor (__init__) method and accessed using self.variable_name.

2. Instance Methods:

- Instance methods are functions that are defined within a class and operate on the object's instance variables.

- They always take self as the first argument, which refers to the instance itself.

- In this example, get_descriptive_name(), read_odometer(), and update_odometer() are instance methods.

- They can access and modify the object's attributes through self.

Final Dish (Output):

```
2023 Toyota Camry
This car has 0 miles on it.
This car has 23500 miles on it.
```

Why is this important?

- **Object State:** Instance variables store the current state or data associated with an object.

- **Object Behavior:** Instance methods define the actions an object can perform, often by manipulating its instance variables.

- **Encapsulation:** Combining data (attributes) and the functions that operate on that data (methods) within a class is a key principle of object-oriented programming (OOP), known as encapsulation.

Recipe 64: Inheritance and Polymorphism

Ingredients (Code):

```python
# Python
class Animal:
    """Represents a generic animal."""
    def __init__(self, name):
        self.name = name

    def speak(self):
        """Makes a generic animal sound."""
        print("Animal sound")


class Dog(Animal):  # Dog inherits from Animal
    """Represents a dog, a type of animal."""

    def speak(self):  # Method overriding (polymorphism)
        """Makes a dog-specific sound."""
        print("Woof!")


class Cat(Animal):  # Cat inherits from Animal
    """Represents a cat, another type of animal."""

    def speak(self):  # Method overriding (polymorphism)
        """Makes a cat-specific sound."""
        print("Meow!")


# Create objects of different animal types
animals = [Animal("Generic Animal"), Dog("Buddy"),
Cat("Whiskers")]

# Polymorphic behavior
for animal in animals:
    animal.speak()  # Calls the correct speak() method
based on the object type
```

Preparation (Explanation):

1. **Inheritance:**

   - **Base Class (Parent Class):** The Animal class serves as the base class. It defines common attributes and methods for all animals.

- **Derived Classes (Child Classes):** The Dog and Cat classes inherit from the Animal class, indicated by the parentheses (Animal). This means they automatically get the name attribute and speak() method from the Animal class.

2. **Method Overriding:**

   - **Polymorphism:** The Dog and Cat classes override the speak() method inherited from the Animal class. They provide their own implementations to make dog-specific ("Woof!") and cat-specific ("Meow!") sounds. This is an example of polymorphism, where objects of different classes can respond to the same method call in their own way.

3. **Creating Objects:**

   - **We create three objects:** one generic Animal, one Dog, and one Cat.

4. **Polymorphic Behaviour:**

   - The loop demonstrates polymorphism in action. When we call the speak() method on each object, Python automatically determines which version of the method to use based on the object's type.

Final Dish (Output):

```
Animal sound
Woof!
Meow!
```

Why is this important?

- **Code Reusability:** Inheritance allows you to reuse code from base classes in derived classes, avoiding duplication.

- **Extensibility:** You can easily extend your code by adding new classes that inherit common features from existing classes.

- **Flexibility:** Polymorphism enables you to write more generic and flexible code that can work with objects of different types seamlessly.

Key Points:

- **super():** The super() function can be used in derived classes to access and call methods from the base class (e.g., super().__init__(name) in the Dog and Cat constructors).

- **isinstance():** Use the isinstance(obj, Class) function to check if an object obj is an instance of a specific class Class or its subclasses.

Recipe 65: Encapsulation (Public, Private, Protected Members)

Ingredients (Code):

```python
# Python
class BankAccount:
    """Represents a bank account with encapsulation."""

    def __init__(self, owner, balance=0):
        """Initializes the account with owner name and
balance."""
        self.owner = owner     # Public member
        self._balance = balance  # Protected member
(single underscore)
        self.__history = []     # Private member (double
underscore)

    def deposit(self, amount):
        """Deposits the given amount into the
account."""
        if amount > 0:
            self._balance += amount
            self.__history.append(f"Deposited $
{amount}")
        else:
            raise ValueError("Deposit amount must be
positive.")

    def withdraw(self, amount):
        """Withdraws the given amount from the
account."""
        if 0 < amount <= self._balance:
            self._balance -= amount
            self.__history.append(f"Withdrew ${amount}")
        else:
            raise ValueError("Invalid withdrawal
amount.")

    def get_balance(self):
        """Returns the current balance."""
        return self._balance

# Example Usage:
my_account = BankAccount("Alice", 1000)
my_account.deposit(500)
my_account.withdraw(200)
print("Balance:", my_account.get_balance())

# Accessing protected member (discouraged, but possible)
print("Balance (using protected access):",
my_account._balance)
```

```
# Trying to access private member (will raise
AttributeError)
# print("Transaction History:", my_account.__history)
```

Preparation (Explanation):

1. **Public Members:**

   - Accessible from anywhere (inside or outside the class).

   - In this example, owner is a public attribute.

2. **Protected Members (Convention):**

   - Conventionally indicated by a single leading underscore (e.g., _balance).

   - Intended to be accessed only within the class or its subclasses.

   - While not strictly enforced by Python, it's a clear signal to other developers not to access them directly from outside.

3. **Private Members (Name Mangling):**

   - Indicated by a double leading underscore (e.g., __history).

   - Python performs name mangling to make these harder to access accidentally from outside the class.

   - The name is changed to _ClassName__attribute, so trying to access __history would become _BankAccount__history. This makes accidental access less likely but doesn't prevent it completely.

- Note: Direct access to private members is generally discouraged, but it's possible using name mangling if absolutely necessary.

Final Dish (Output):

```
Balance: 1300
Balance (using protected access): 1300
```

(The line trying to access __history directly would raise an AttributeError.)

Why is this important?

- **Data Protection:** Encapsulation protects the internal state of an object by restricting direct access to its attributes. This prevents accidental changes and makes your code more robust.

- **Data Hiding:** Private members hide implementation details, allowing you to modify the internal workings of a class without affecting how external code interacts with it.

- **Interface Control:** You can define a public interface (methods like deposit, withdraw, get_balance) that controls how other code interacts with the object. This makes your code more maintainable and less prone to unexpected side effects.

14. Datetime Module:

Recipe 66: Getting Current Date and Time

Ingredients (Code):

```python
# Python
from datetime import datetime

# Get the current date and time
now = datetime.now()

# Print the current date and time
print(f"Current Date and Time: {now}")

# Extract individual components
year = now.year
month = now.month
day = now.day
hour = now.hour
minute = now.minute
second = now.second
microsecond = now.microsecond

print("Year:", year)
print("Month:", month)
print("Day:", day)
print("Hour:", hour)
print("Minute:", minute)
print("Second:", second)
print("Microsecond:", microsecond)
```

Preparation (Explanation):

1. **Import datetime:**

   - From the datetime module, import the datetime class. This class is used to represent a specific point in time.

2. **Get Current Date and Time (datetime.now()):**

   - **now = datetime.now():** This line gets the current local date and time and stores it in the variable now. This includes the year, month, day, hour, minute, second, and microsecond.

3. **Print the Current Date and Time:**

   - **print(f"Current Date and Time: {now}"):** This line simply prints the now object, which by default will display a string representation of the date and time in the format: YYYY-MM-DD HH:MM:SS.mmmmmm.

4. **Extract Individual Components:**

   - You can access individual components of the datetime object using its attributes:

     - **now.year:** The year (e.g., 2024).

     - **now.month:** The month (1-12).

     - **now.day:** The day of the month (1-31).

     - **now.hour:** The hour (0-23).

     - **now.minute:** The minute (0-59).

     - **now.second:** The second (0-59).

     - **now.microsecond:** The microsecond (0-999999).

Final Dish (Output):

```
Current Date and Time: 2024-06-12 17:18:34.711996
Year: 2024
Month: 6
Day: 12
Hour: 17
Minute: 18
Second: 34
Microsecond: 711996
```

(The output will vary based on your current date and time.)

Why is this important?

- **Timestamps:** Getting the current time is essential for creating timestamps in log files, tracking events, or measuring the duration of processes.

- **Scheduling:** Date and time information is crucial for scheduling tasks, setting reminders, or calculating time differences.

- **Data Analysis:** Time stamps are often included in data sets to analyze trends over time or create time-based reports.

Recipe 67: Formatting Dates and Times

Ingredients (Code):

```python
# Python
from datetime import datetime

now = datetime.now()

# Common formatting directives
print("ISO 8601:", now.isoformat())
# YYYY-MM-DDTHH:MM:SS.ffffff
print("Default:", now)
# YYYY-MM-DD HH:MM:SS.ffffff
print("Custom 1:", now.strftime("%Y-%m-%d"))
# YYYY-MM-DD
print("Custom 2:", now.strftime("%A, %B %d, %Y"))
# Day of week, Month Day, Year
print("Custom 3:", now.strftime("%I:%M %p"))
# Hour:Minute AM/PM
print("Custom 4:", now.strftime("%d/%m/%y %H:%M"))
# DD/MM/YY HH:MM (24-hour)
print("Custom 5(IST):", now.strftime("%d-%m-%Y, %I:%M %p
%Z"))   # DD-MM-YYYY, HH:MM AM/PM IST
```

Preparation (Explanation):

1. **Get Current Date and Time (datetime.now()):**

   - Retrieves the current date and time (including year, month, day, hour, minute, second, and microsecond) and stores it in the now variable.

2. **Formatting Directives:**

   - **%Y:** Year with century (e.g., 2024)

   - **%y:** Year without century (e.g., 24)

   - **%m:** Month as a zero-padded decimal number (e.g., 06)

   - **%B:** Full month name (e.g., June)

   - **%d:** Day of the month as a zero-padded decimal (e.g., 12)

- **%A:** Full weekday name (e.g., Wednesday)

- **%H:** Hour (24-hour clock) as a zero-padded decimal (e.g., 17)

- **%I:** Hour (12-hour clock) as a zero-padded decimal (e.g., 05)

- **%M:** Minute as a zero-padded decimal (e.g., 20)

- **%S:** Second as a zero-padded decimal (e.g., 30)

- **%p:** Locale's AM/PM (e.g., PM)

- **%Z:** Time zone name (e.g., IST)

3. **Formatting Methods:**

- **isoformat():** Returns the date and time in the standard ISO 8601 format (YYYY-MM-DDTHH:MM:SS.ffffff).

- **strftime(format):** This method allows custom formatting. You pass a format string containing directives (%Y, %m, etc.) that specify how you want the date and time components to be represented in the output string.

Final Dish (Output):

```
ISO 8601: 2024-06-12T17:20:13.414314
Default: 2024-06-12 17:20:13.414314
Custom 1: 2024-06-12
Custom 2: Wednesday, June 12, 2024
Custom 3: 05:20 PM
Custom 4: 12/06/24 17:20
Custom 5(IST): 12-06-2024, 05:20 PM IST
```

(The output will vary based on your current date, time, and location.)

Why is this important?

- **Readability:** Formatting dates and times makes them easier for humans to read and understand.

- **Presentation:** You can use formatting to display dates and times in a way that matches your application's or user's preferences.

- **Localization:** The strftime() method supports locale-specific formatting, adapting the output to different regions or languages.

Recipe 68: Timedeltas (Calculating Time Differences)

Ingredients (Code):

```python
# Python
from datetime import datetime, timedelta

# Get the current date and time
now = datetime.now()
print(f"Current time: {now}")

# Create a timedelta representing 2 weeks and 3 days
time_difference = timedelta(weeks=2, days=3)

# Calculate future time by adding timedelta
future_time = now + time_difference
print(f"Future time: {future_time}")

# Calculate past time by subtracting timedelta
past_time = now - time_difference
print(f"Past time: {past_time}")

# Calculate the time difference between two dates
new_year = datetime(2025, 1, 1)  # New Year's Day 2025
time_until_new_year = new_year - now
print(f"Time until New Year's Day 2025:
{time_until_new_year}")

# Get the total seconds in the timedelta
total_seconds = time_until_new_year.total_seconds()
print(f"Total seconds until New Year's Day 2025:
{total_seconds}")
```

Preparation (Explanation):

1. **Import timedelta:**

   - Import the timedelta class from the datetime module. This class represents a duration of time (difference between two dates or times).

2. **Create a timedelta Object:**

   - **timedelta(weeks=2, days=3):** Creates a timedelta object representing a duration of 2 weeks and 3 days. You can specify durations in various units like days, seconds, microseconds, milliseconds, minutes, hours, weeks.

3. **Add/Subtract Timedeltas to/from Datetime:**

- **now + time_difference:** Adds the time_difference to the current time (now), calculating a point in the future.

- **now - time_difference:** Subtracts the time_difference from the current time, calculating a point in the past.

4. **Calculate Time Differences:**

- **new_year - now:** Calculates the time difference between New Year's Day 2025 and the current time. The result is another timedelta object.

5. **Get Total Seconds:**

- **time_until_new_year.total_seconds():** Returns the total number of seconds in the time_until_new_year timedelta.

Final Dish (Output):

```
Current time: 2024-06-12 17:21:41.304712
Future time: 2024-07-02 17:21:41.304712
Past time: 2024-05-21 17:21:41.304712
Time until New Year's Day 2025: 172 days, 6:38:18.695288
Total seconds until New Year's Day 2025: 14874918.695288
```

(The output will vary based on your current date and time.)

Why is this important?

- **Time Calculations:** timedelta objects are essential for calculating durations, time differences, and future/past dates and times.

- **Scheduling:** You can use timedeltas to schedule tasks to run at specific intervals or to calculate deadlines.

- **Data Analysis:** When working with time-series data, timedeltas help you determine the elapsed time between events or analyze trends over time.

Recipe 69: Working with Time Zones

Ingredients (Code):

```python
# Python
import datetime
import pytz  # Install this module with pip: pip install
pytz

# Get current time in UTC (Coordinated Universal Time)
utc_now = datetime.datetime.now(pytz.utc)
print(f"Current time in UTC: {utc_now}")

# Convert UTC time to a specific time zone (e.g., EST)
est_timezone = pytz.timezone('US/Eastern')
est_time = utc_now.astimezone(est_timezone)
print(f"Current time in EST: {est_time}")

# Convert to IST timezone
ist_timezone = pytz.timezone('Asia/Kolkata')
ist_time = utc_now.astimezone(ist_timezone)
print(f"Current time in IST: {ist_time}")

# List available timezones (a small selection)
some_timezones = ['US/Pacific', 'Europe/London', 'Asia/
Tokyo', 'Australia/Sydney']
print("\nSome available timezones:")
for tz in some_timezones:
    print(tz)

# Convert a naive (timezone-unaware) datetime to a
specific timezone
naive_datetime = datetime.datetime(2024, 6, 12, 10, 30)
# June 12, 2024 at 10:30 AM
localized_datetime =
est_timezone.localize(naive_datetime)
print("\nNaive datetime:", naive_datetime)
print("Localized datetime (EST):", localized_datetime)
```

Preparation (Explanation):

1. **Import Required Modules:**

    - **datetime:** Provides classes for working with dates and times.

    - **pytz:** A third-party module (install using pip install pytz) that provides a comprehensive database of time zones and timezone-aware datetime objects.

2. **Get Current Time in UTC:**

   - **datetime.datetime.now(pytz.utc):** Retrieves the current date and time in Coordinated Universal Time (UTC), which is the standard reference time zone.

3. **Convert to Specific Time Zone:**

   - **pytz.timezone('US/Eastern'):** Creates a timezone object for Eastern Standard Time (EST).

   - **utc_now.astimezone(est_timezone):** Converts the utc_now datetime to EST time.

4. **List Available Time Zones:**

   - **pytz.all_timezones:** A list of all available time zone names. (This list is quite long, so we're showing a small sample here.)

5. **Localize Naive Datetime:**

   - **datetime.datetime(2024, 6, 12, 10, 30):** Creates a naive datetime object (no timezone information).

   - **est_timezone.localize(naive_datetime):** Attaches the EST timezone information to the naive datetime.

Final Dish (Output):

```
Current time in UTC: 2024-06-12 17:22:18.428505+00:00
Current time in EST: 2024-06-12 13:22:18.428505-04:00
Current time in IST: 2024-06-12 22:52:18.428505+05:30

Some available timezones:
```

```
US/Pacific
Europe/London
Asia/Tokyo
Australia/Sydney

Naive datetime: 2024-06-12 10:30:00
Localized datetime (EST): 2024-06-12 10:30:00-04:00
```
(The output will vary based on your current time and location.)

Why is this important?

- **Global Applications:** If your software deals with users or events in different locations, handling time zones correctly is essential to avoid confusion and errors in scheduling, logging, or displaying time-related information.

- **Data Accuracy:** Time zone awareness ensures that your data is consistent and accurately reflects the time it was created or recorded, regardless of the user's location.

Recipe 70: Scheduling Tasks (Using datetime and time)

Ingredients (Code):

```python
# Python
import datetime
import time

def task_to_run():
    """The function that will be scheduled to run."""
    print(f"Task running at {datetime.datetime.now()}")

# Schedule the task to run in 5 seconds
schedule_time = datetime.datetime.now() + datetime.timedelta(seconds=5)

# Wait until the scheduled time
while datetime.datetime.now() < schedule_time:
    time.sleep(1)  # Sleep for 1 second to avoid busy waiting

# Run the task
task_to_run()
```

Preparation (Explanation):

1. **Import Modules:**

   - **datetime:** Used for handling date and time objects.

   - **time:** Provides functions for working with time, including sleep().

2. **Define the Task Function (task_to_run()):**

   - This function represents the task you want to schedule. In this example, it simply prints the current time when it's executed. You can replace this with any code you want to run at the scheduled time.

3. **Calculate Scheduled Time:**

- **schedule_time = datetime.datetime.now() + datetime.timedelta(seconds=5):**

  - **datetime.datetime.now():** Gets the current time.

  - **datetime.timedelta(seconds=5):** Creates a time delta object representing a duration of 5 seconds.

  - Adding the timedelta to the current time calculates the time 5 seconds in the future.

4. **Wait Loop:**

   - **while datetime.datetime.now() < schedule_time:** This loop continues until the current time (datetime.datetime.now()) is equal to or greater than the schedule_time.

   - **time.sleep(1):** Makes the loop pause for 1 second before checking the time again. This prevents your program from using excessive CPU resources while waiting (known as "busy waiting").

5. **Execute the Task:**

   - Once the while loop condition becomes False (meaning the scheduled time has arrived), the task_to_run() function is called.

Final Dish (Output):

```
Task running at 2024-06-12 17:27:13.681069
```
(The exact time in the output will vary)

Why is this important?

- **Task Automation:** This approach lets you automate tasks to run at specific times or intervals without requiring external scheduling tools.

- **Customizable Schedules:** You can easily adjust the schedule by changing the timedelta value (e.g., to run the task every hour, every day, or at a specific time of day).

- **Simple and Flexible:** While this is a basic scheduling mechanism, it's suitable for many tasks and can be customized for more complex scenarios.

Key Points:

- **Precision Limitations:** The accuracy of this method is limited by the resolution of your system clock and the overhead of the sleep() function. For very precise timing, you might need to explore alternative scheduling libraries or tools.

- **Alternative Libraries:** For more advanced scheduling needs, consider using libraries like schedule or APScheduler, which offer features like recurring tasks, event-based triggers, and more sophisticated time calculations.

15. Advanced Topics:

Recipe 71: Context Managers (with statement)

Ingredients (Code):

```python
# Python
# File handling using a context manager
with open("example.txt", "w") as file:
    file.write("This is some text written to the file.
\n")
print("File written and automatically closed.")

# Custom context manager (timer)
import time

class Timer:
    def __enter__(self):
        self.start_time = time.time()
        return self

    def __exit__(self, exc_type, exc_value, traceback):
        end_time = time.time()
        elapsed_time = end_time - self.start_time
        print(f"Elapsed time: {elapsed_time:.2f}
seconds")

# Using the custom timer
with Timer() as timer:
    # Simulate some work taking time
    time.sleep(2.5)
    print("Work inside the context manager completed.")
```

Preparation (Explanation):

1. **What Are Context Managers?**

    - Context managers are objects that define how to set up and tear down a context for a block of code.

    - They are used with the with statement to ensure that resources are properly managed.

2. **with Statement:**

    - **with expression as target:**

- The expression is evaluated to obtain a context manager object.

- The context manager's __enter__() method is called. The return value of __enter__() (if any) is assigned to the target variable.

- The code block within the with statement is executed.

- The context manager's __exit__() method is called, regardless of whether an exception occurred within the block.

3. **File Handling Example:**

   - **open("example.txt", "w"):** Opens the file in write mode and returns a file object.

   - This file object is used as a context manager. It ensures the file is closed automatically after the block ends, even if an exception occurs.

4. **Custom Context Manager (Timer):**

   - The Timer class defines __enter__ and __exit__ methods to create a timer context.

   - **__enter__**: Starts the timer and returns the Timer object itself.

   - **__exit__**: Stops the timer and calculates the elapsed time.

Final Dish (Output):

```
File written and automatically closed.
Work inside the context manager completed.
Elapsed time: 2.50 seconds
```

Why is this important?

- **Resource Management:** Context managers make resource management (e.g., file handling, network connections, database transactions) more convenient and reliable. They ensure resources are properly closed or released, even in the face of errors.

- **Cleaner Code:** The with statement eliminates the need for explicit try...finally blocks for cleanup, leading to cleaner, more readable code.

- **Flexibility:** You can create custom context managers to manage any kind of resource or context in your code.

Recipe 72: Iterators and Generators

Ingredients (Code):

```python
# Python
# Iterator Example
class MyRange:
    """A simple custom iterator that mimics the range()
function."""

    def __init__(self, start, stop):
        self.current = start
        self.stop = stop

    def __iter__(self):
        return self

    def __next__(self):
        if self.current < self.stop:
            num = self.current
            self.current += 1
            return num
        else:
            raise StopIteration

# Using the custom iterator
my_range = MyRange(1, 5)
for num in my_range:
    print(num)

print("-" * 10) # Add separator


# Generator Example (using yield)
def my_generator(n):
    """A simple generator that yields numbers from 0 to
n-1."""
    for i in range(n):
        yield i

# Using the generator
for num in my_generator(5):
    print(num)
```

Preparation (Explanation):

1. Iterators:

- **Purpose:** Iterators are objects that allow you to traverse
  through a sequence of elements one at a time. They

maintain an internal state to keep track of the current position.

- **Iterator Protocol:** To be an iterator, an object must implement two special methods:

  - **__iter__**: Returns the iterator object itself.

  - **__next__**: Returns the next element in the sequence and updates the iterator's state. When there are no more items, it raises the StopIteration exception.

- **Example (MyRange):**

  - This custom class defines an iterator similar to Python's built-in range().

  - **__init__**: Initializes the current value (starting point) and stop value (ending point).

  - **__iter__**: Returns the iterator object (self).

  - **__next__**: Returns the next value and increments current. If current reaches stop, it raises StopIteration.

2. Generators:

- **Simplified Iterators:** Generators are a concise way to create iterators using functions.

- **yield Keyword:** Instead of return, generators use the yield keyword to produce the next value in the sequence.

- **Lazy Evaluation:** Generators are lazy, meaning they generate values on the fly as they are requested, rather than storing all values in memory at once.

- **Example (my_generator):**

  - The function my_generator(n) yields values from 0 up to n-1.

  - When the for loop requests the next value, the generator function resumes from where it left off, thanks to the yield keyword.

Final Dish (Output):

```
1
2
3
4
----------
0
1
2
3
4
```

Why is this important?

- **Memory Efficiency:** Iterators and generators are excellent for handling large datasets or infinite sequences, as they only generate elements when needed, saving memory.

- **Lazy Evaluation:** Lazy evaluation can improve performance by avoiding unnecessary computations.

- **Readability:** Generators often lead to cleaner and more readable code for tasks that involve iterating over data.

- **Iterable Objects:** Many built-in Python types (lists, dictionaries, strings, etc.) are already iterable, meaning you can use them directly in for loops without needing to create explicit iterators.

Recipe 73: Decorators (Modifying Function Behavior)

Ingredients (Code):

```python
# Python
# Decorator function
def my_decorator(func):
    """
    This is a decorator function that takes a function
    as input and returns a modified version of it.
    """
    def wrapper(*args, **kwargs):
        print("Something is happening before the
function is called.")
        result = func(*args, **kwargs)
        print("Something is happening after the function
is called.")
        return result
    return wrapper

# Function to be decorated
@my_decorator
def say_hello(name):
    """Greets a person by name."""
    print(f"Hello, {name}!")
    return f"Hello, {name}!"  # Example return value

# Calling the decorated function
return_value = say_hello("Alice")
print(return_value)
```

Preparation (Explanation):

1. **Decorator Function:**

   - my_decorator is a function that takes another function (func) as input.

   - Inside my_decorator, there's a nested function called wrapper. This wrapper function:

     - Accepts any number of positional (*args) and keyword (**kwargs) arguments.

     - Executes some code before calling the original function func.

- Calls the original function func with the passed arguments.

- Executes some code after calling the original function.

- Returns the result of the original function.

2. **Decorator Syntax (@my_decorator):**

- The @ symbol before my_decorator indicates that say_hello should be "decorated" by my_decorator.

- This is equivalent to writing:

```Python
say_hello = my_decorator(say_hello)
```
- The decorated function (say_hello) is replaced with the wrapper function returned by the decorator.

Final Dish (Output):

```
Something is happening before the function is called.
Hello, Alice!
Something is happening after the function is called.
Hello, Alice!
```

Why is this important?

- **Modifying Behavior:** Decorators provide a way to modify the behavior of existing functions without changing their code directly.

- **Code Reusability:** You can apply the same decorator to multiple functions to add common functionality (e.g., logging, timing, input validation).

- **Clean Syntax:** The @ syntax is a concise and readable way to use decorators.

Key Points:

- Decorators can be nested (applied multiple times to a function).

- Decorators can take arguments themselves.

- The standard library includes several built-in decorators (e.g., @classmethod, @staticmethod, @property).

Recipe 74: Property Decorators (Getters, Setters, Deleters)

Ingredients (Code):

```python
# Python
class Employee:
    """Represents an employee with name and salary."""
    def __init__(self, name, salary):
        self._name = name
        self._salary = salary

    @property  # Getter
    def name(self):
        """Gets the employee's name."""
        return self._name

    @name.setter  # Setter
    def name(self, new_name):
        """Sets the employee's name, enforcing
capitalization."""
        if not isinstance(new_name, str):
            raise TypeError("Name must be a string.")
        self._name = new_name.capitalize()  # Ensure
first letter is capitalized

    @property  # Getter
    def salary(self):
        """Gets the employee's salary."""
        return self._salary

    @salary.setter  # Setter
    def salary(self, new_salary):
        """Sets the employee's salary, ensuring it's not
negative."""
        if new_salary < 0:
            raise ValueError("Salary cannot be
negative.")
        self._salary = new_salary

    @salary.deleter  # Deleter
    def salary(self):
        """Deletes the employee's salary information."""
        del self._salary

# Example Usage:
emp = Employee("alice johnson", 50000)
print(emp.name)  # Access using property (calls getter)

emp.name = "bob smith"  # Modify using property (calls
setter)
print(emp.name)
```

```
print(emp.salary)
emp.salary = 60000
print(emp.salary)

del emp.salary   # Delete salary information (calls
deleter)
# print(emp.salary)   # This would now raise an
AttributeError
```

Preparation (Explanation):

1. Property Decorators:

- **@property:** Turns a method into a "getter" for an attribute. Accessing emp.name actually calls this method.

- **@<property_name>.setter:** Defines a "setter" method to modify the attribute's value. Assigning to emp.name triggers this method.

- **@<property_name>.deleter:** Defines a "deleter" method to remove the attribute. Using del emp.salary calls this method.

2. Why Use Property Decorators?

- **Encapsulation:** Control how attributes are accessed and modified.

- **Validation:** Enforce rules or constraints on attribute values (e.g., capitalization of names, non-negative salaries).

- **Abstraction:** Hide implementation details of how data is stored and retrieved. Users interact with the attributes as if they were normal variables, but the getter/setter methods handle the logic behind the scenes.

3. Example (Employee Class):

- **name Property:** The getter returns the employee's name, and the setter ensures proper capitalization.

- **salary Property:** The getter returns the salary, the setter prevents negative values, and the deleter removes the salary information.

Final Dish (Output):

```
Alice Johnson
Bob Smith
50000
60000
```

(The last line attempting to print emp.salary would raise an AttributeError because the salary has been deleted.)

Important Note:

- In Python, it's a convention to use a single underscore prefix for "protected" attributes (e.g., _name, _salary). This indicates that they shouldn't be accessed directly from outside the class, although Python doesn't strictly enforce this.

Recipe 75: Multithreading and Concurrency

Ingredients (Code):

```python
# Python
import threading
import time

# Function to be executed in threads
def task(name):
    """Simulates a task taking some time to complete."""
    print(f"Thread {name}: starting")
    time.sleep(2)  # Simulate work
    print(f"Thread {name}: finishing")

# Create and start multiple threads
if __name__ == "__main__": # Ensure this code runs only
when this file is the main program
  threads = []
  for i in range(3):
      thread = threading.Thread(target=task, args=(i,))
      threads.append(thread)
      thread.start()

  # Wait for all threads to complete (optional)
  for thread in threads:
      thread.join()
  print("All threads finished.")
```

Preparation (Explanation):

1. **Threading Module:**

    - **import threading:** Imports the threading module, which provides tools for working with threads.

2. **task Function:**

    - This function represents the task you want to run concurrently.

    - time.sleep(2) simulates the task taking 2 seconds to complete.

3. **Creating Threads (threading.Thread):**

- **threading.Thread(target=task, args=(i,)):**

  - **target:** The function to be executed in the thread (task).

  - **args:** A tuple containing arguments to pass to the target function. Here, we pass the thread's index (i) to identify it in the output.

4. **Starting Threads (thread.start()):**

   - **thread.start():** This method starts the thread, allowing it to run concurrently with the main program and other threads.

5. **Joining Threads (thread.join() - Optional):**

   - **thread.join():** Waits for a thread to finish its execution. The main program will pause until the joined thread completes.

   - The loop iterates over all threads and joins them to ensure the main program doesn't exit before all tasks are finished.

Final Dish (Output):

```
Thread 0: starting
Thread 1: starting
Thread 2: starting
Thread 0: finishing
Thread 1: finishing
Thread 2: finishing
All threads finished.
```

(The order of thread output might vary slightly due to the nature of concurrency.)

Why is this important?

- **Concurrency:** Threads enable your program to perform multiple tasks concurrently, potentially improving performance, responsiveness, and resource utilization.

- **Parallelism (Sometimes):** If your computer has multiple CPU cores, threads might even run in parallel, truly executing simultaneously. (In Python, this is limited by the Global Interpreter Lock (GIL) for CPython implementation, but can be achieved using multiprocessing for CPU-bound tasks.)

- **Responsiveness:** Tasks that take a long time (like network requests or file I/O) can be offloaded to background threads, allowing the main program to remain responsive to user input.

Key Points:

- **Shared Resources:** Threads share memory space, so you need to be careful with how they access and modify shared data (consider using locks or other synchronization mechanisms to avoid race conditions).

- **Not Always Faster:** Threading isn't a magic solution for making everything faster. It adds overhead, and in some cases, it might even slow things down. Use it judiciously for tasks that benefit from concurrency.

16. Additional Libraries/Topics:

Recipe 76: Regular Expressions (re Module)

Ingredients (Code):

```python
# Python
import re

text = "My email address is john.doe@example.com, and my
phone number is +1-555-123-4567."

# Basic pattern matching
email_pattern = r"\b[A-Za-z0-9._%+-]+@[A-Za-z0-9.-]+\.
[A-Za-z]{2,}\b"
phone_pattern = r"\+\d{1,3}-\d{3}-\d{3}-\d{4}"

email_match = re.search(email_pattern, text)
phone_match = re.search(phone_pattern, text)

if email_match:
    print(f"Email found: {email_match.group()}")
else:
    print("No email found.")

if phone_match:
    print(f"Phone number found: {phone_match.group()}")
else:
    print("No phone number found.")

# Finding all matches
all_numbers = re.findall(r"\d+", text)  # Find all
sequences of digits
print(f"All numbers found: {all_numbers}")

# Substitution (replace)
modified_text = re.sub(r"\d", "X", text)  # Replace all
digits with "X"
print(f"Modified text: {modified_text}")
```

Preparation (Explanation):

1. **Import the re Module:**

   - **import re:** This line brings in the regular expression module, which provides functions for working with patterns in text.

2. **Patterns:**

- **email_pattern:**

    - **\b:** Word boundary (start or end of a word)

    - **[A-Za-z0-9._%+-]+:** One or more alphanumeric characters, dots, underscores, percent signs, plus or minus signs.

    - **@:** Literal "@" symbol

    - **[A-Za-z0-9.-]+:** One or more alphanumeric characters, dots, or hyphens.

    - **\.:** Literal dot (escaped with backslash)

    - **[A-Za-z]{2,}:** Two or more letters (for the top-level domain)

- phone_pattern:

    - **\+\d{1,3}:** A plus sign followed by one to three digits (country code)

    - **-:** Literal hyphen

    - **\d{3}:** Three digits (area code)

    - **-:** Literal hyphen

    - **\d{3}:** Three digits

    - **-:** Literal hyphen

    - **\d{4}:** Four digits

3. **Searching with re.search(pattern, string):**

- Finds the first match of the pattern in the string.

- Returns a match object containing information about the match, or None if no match is found.

4. **Finding All Matches with re.findall(pattern, string):**

   - Returns a list of all non-overlapping matches of the pattern in the string.

   - In the example, it finds all sequences of one or more digits (\d+).

5. **Replacing with re.sub(pattern, repl, string):**

   - Replaces all occurrences of the pattern in the string with the repl string.

   - In the example, it replaces all digits with "X".

Final Dish (Output):

```
Email found: john.doe@example.com
Phone number found: +1-555-123-4567
All numbers found: ['1', '555', '123', '4567']
Modified text: My email address is john.doe@example.com,
and my phone number is +X-XXX-XXX-XXXX.
```

Why is this important?

- **Powerful Text Processing:** Regular expressions enable complex text searching, matching, and manipulation that would be difficult or tedious with basic string methods.

- **Data Extraction:** You can extract structured information (like email addresses, phone numbers, or dates) from unstructured text.

- **Data Validation:** Regular expressions are great for validating user input to ensure it conforms to specific formats.

Recipe 77: Collections Module (deque, Counter, defaultdict, etc.)

Ingredients (Code):

```python
# Python
from collections import deque, Counter, defaultdict

# deque (Double-ended queue)
dq = deque([1, 2, 3])
dq.append(4)      # Add to the right side
dq.appendleft(0) # Add to the left side
print(f"Deque: {dq}")
dq.pop()          # Remove from the right side
dq.popleft()      # Remove from the left side
print(f"Deque after pops: {dq}")

print("-" * 10) # Add separator

# Counter (Counts occurrences of elements)
text = "hello world this is a test hello"
word_counts = Counter(text.split())
print(f"Word Counts: {word_counts}")
print(f"Most common word: {word_counts.most_common(1)}")

print("-" * 10) # Add separator

# defaultdict (Dictionary with default values for
missing keys)
fruit_counts = defaultdict(int)  # Default value is 0
(for counting)
fruits = ["apple", "banana", "apple", "orange",
"banana", "apple"]
for fruit in fruits:
    fruit_counts[fruit] += 1
print(f"Fruit Counts: {fruit_counts}")
```

Preparation (Explanation):

1. **Deque (deque):**

   - **Purpose:** A double-ended queue allows fast append and pop operations from both ends. Think of it like a line where you can add or remove people from either the front or the back.

   - **Methods:**

     - **append(x):** Add x to the right side.

225

- **appendleft(x):** Add x to the left side.

- **pop():** Remove and return an element from the right side.

- **popleft():** Remove and return an element from the left side.

2. **Counter (Counter):**

   - **Purpose:** A dictionary-like container that keeps track of the counts of hashable objects.

   - **Example:** In this recipe, we count the occurrences of each word in a sentence.

   - **Methods:**

     - **most_common(n):** Returns a list of the n most common elements and their counts.

3. **Defaultdict (defaultdict):**

   - **Purpose:** A dictionary that provides a default value for keys that do not exist, avoiding KeyError exceptions.

   - **Example:** We use defaultdict(int) to count fruits, as it initializes counts to 0 automatically for any new fruit encountered.

Final Dish (Output):

```
Deque: deque([0, 1, 2, 3, 4])
Deque after pops: deque([1, 2, 3])
----------
Word Counts: Counter({'hello': 2, 'world': 1, 'this': 1,
'is': 1, 'a': 1, 'test': 1})
Most common word: [('hello', 2)]
----------
Fruit Counts: defaultdict(<class 'int'>, {'apple': 3,
'banana': 2, 'orange': 1})
```

Why is this important?

- **Specialized Containers:** The collections module offers data structures that are tailored for specific use cases, often more convenient or efficient than basic lists or dictionaries.

- **Enhanced Functionality:** These containers provide additional methods and features to streamline common operations.

- **Improved Readability:** Using the right container can make your code more expressive and easier to understand.

Recipe 78: Web Scraping (requests, BeautifulSoup)

Ingredients (Code):

```python
# Python
import requests
from bs4 import BeautifulSoup

# Target website (replace with the actual URL you want
to scrape)
url = "https://www.example.com"

# Fetch the HTML content using requests
response = requests.get(url)

# Check if the request was successful
if response.status_code == 200:
    # Parse the HTML content using BeautifulSoup
    soup = BeautifulSoup(response.text, 'html.parser')

    # Example: Extract all links from the page
    links = []
    for link in soup.find_all('a'):  # Find all anchor
tags (<a>)
        links.append(link.get('href'))  # Get the 'href'
attribute (link URL)
    print(links)

    # Example: Extract the title of the page
    title = soup.title.string
    print("Title:", title)
else:
    print(f"Request failed with status code:
{response.status_code}")
```

Preparation (Explanation):

1. **Import Libraries:**

    - **requests:** Used for sending HTTP requests to websites and retrieving their content.

    - **BeautifulSoup:** Used for parsing (analyzing) HTML and XML documents, making it easier to extract specific information.

2. **Fetch HTML Content:**

- **requests.get(url):** Sends a GET request to the specified url and returns a Response object.

3. **Check Response Status Code:**

   - **response.status_code:** This attribute of the Response object tells you whether the request was successful (200 means OK).

4. **Parse HTML with BeautifulSoup:**

   - **BeautifulSoup(response.text, 'html.parser'):** Creates a BeautifulSoup object (soup) by parsing the HTML content of the response using the html.parser.

5. **Extract Information:**

   - **soup.find_all('a'):** Finds all anchor tags (<a>) in the HTML.

   - **link.get('href'):** Gets the value of the href attribute (the link URL) for each link.

   - **soup.title.string:** Extracts the text content of the <title> tag (the title of the webpage).

Final Dish (Output):

```
['/link1', '/link2', '/link3', ...]
Title: Example Domain
```
(The exact output will vary depending on the structure of the website you're scraping.)

Why is this important?

- **Data Gathering:** Web scraping is a powerful technique for gathering data from websites that don't offer APIs or easy ways to export data.

- **Automation:** You can automate tasks that involve repetitive interaction with websites.

- **Research and Analysis:** Web scraping is used extensively for research, market analysis, price comparison, and more.

Ethical Considerations:

- **Robots.txt:** Always check a website's robots.txt file to see if scraping is allowed.

- **Respectful Crawling:** Avoid overloading a website with too many requests. Use delays between requests if needed.

- **Data Usage:** Be mindful of how you use the scraped data, especially if it contains personal or sensitive information.

Recipe 79: GUI Development (Tkinter)

Ingredients (Code):

```python
# Python
import tkinter as tk

def on_click():
    """Handles button clicks."""
    label.config(text="Button clicked!")

# Create main window
window = tk.Tk()
window.title("Simple GUI")

# Create a label widget
label = tk.Label(window, text="Hello, Tkinter!")
label.pack(padx=20, pady=20)  # Add padding

# Create a button widget
button = tk.Button(window, text="Click Me",
command=on_click)
button.pack()

# Start the GUI event loop
window.mainloop()
```

Preparation (Explanation):

1. **Import Tkinter (import tkinter as tk):**

   - Imports the Tkinter module and gives it the alias tk for easier reference.

2. **Create Main Window (window = tk.Tk()):**

   - Creates the main application window.

   - **window.title("Simple GUI"):** Sets the title of the window.

3. **Create Label Widget (label = tk.Label(...)):**

   - Creates a label to display text.

   - **window:** Specifies the parent widget (the main window in this case).

- **text:** Sets the initial text of the label.
- **label.pack(padx=20, pady=20):**
  - Adds the label to the window and uses the pack geometry manager to arrange it.
  - padx and pady add padding (empty space) around the label.

4. **Create Button Widget (button = tk.Button(...)):**
   - Creates a button.
   - **command=on_click:** Specifies the function to call (on_click) when the button is clicked.

5. **on_click() Function:**
   - This function is called when the button is clicked.
   - **label.config(text="Button clicked!"):** Changes the text of the label widget.

6. **Start the GUI Event Loop (window.mainloop()):**
   - This line starts the Tkinter event loop.
   - The event loop listens for user interactions (like button clicks) and responds accordingly.
   - Your program will run indefinitely until the user closes the window.

Final Dish (Output):

```
This code will open a window with a label that says
"Hello, Tkinter!" and a button labeled "Click Me." When
you click the button, the label's text will change to
"Button clicked!".
```

Why is this important?

- **Graphical Interfaces:** Tkinter is a standard Python library for creating desktop GUI applications. It allows you to build interactive programs with buttons, text boxes, menus, and more.

- **Event-Driven Programming:** GUI programming is event-driven, meaning your code reacts to events like button clicks, mouse movements, or keyboard presses.

- **Widely Used:** Tkinter is cross-platform (works on Windows, macOS, and Linux) and relatively simple to learn, making it a popular choice for building basic GUIs in Python.

Recipe 80: Data Analysis (Pandas, NumPy)

Ingredients (Code):

```python
# Python
import pandas as pd
import numpy as np

# Create a DataFrame (tabular data structure)
data = {'Name': ['Alice', 'Bob', 'Charlie'],
        'Age': [25, 32, 40],
        'City': ['New York', 'London', 'Paris']}
df = pd.DataFrame(data)

# Display the DataFrame
print("Original DataFrame:")
print(df)

# Accessing Data
print("\nAges:")
print(df['Age'])   # Access a single column
print(df.loc[1])   # Access a row by index
print(df.iloc[0:2, 1:3])  # Access a slice (rows 0-1,
columns 1-2)

# Filtering Data
filtered_df = df[df['Age'] > 30]
print("\nPeople older than 30:")
print(filtered_df)

# Basic Statistics
print("\nAverage Age:", df['Age'].mean())
print("Maximum Age:", df['Age'].max())

# NumPy Operations
ages = df['Age'].to_numpy()   # Convert to NumPy array
print("\nAges as NumPy array:", ages)

# Calculate sum and standard deviation
sum_of_ages = np.sum(ages)
std_dev_ages = np.std(ages)

print(f"Sum of ages: {sum_of_ages}")
print(f"Standard Deviation of ages: {std_dev_ages:.2f}")
# Format to 2 decimals
```

Preparation (Explanation):

   1. **Import Libraries:**

- **import pandas as pd:** Imports the Pandas library, typically aliased as pd.

- **import numpy as np:** Imports the NumPy library, typically aliased as np.

2. **Create DataFrame:**

   - A DataFrame is a 2-dimensional labeled data structure (like a table or spreadsheet).

   - You can create one from dictionaries, lists, or other data sources.

3. **Accessing Data:**

   - **df['Age']:** Accesses the Age column.

   - **df.loc[1]:** Accesses the row at index 1.

   - **df.iloc[0:2, 1:3]:** Accesses rows 0 and 1, and columns 1 and 2.

4. **Filtering Data:**

   - **df[df['Age'] > 30]:** Creates a new DataFrame containing only rows where Age is greater than 30.

5. **Basic Statistics:**

   - **df['Age'].mean():** Calculates the mean (average) age.

   - **df['Age'].max():** Calculates the maximum age.

6. **NumPy Operations:**

   - **df['Age'].to_numpy():** Converts the Age column to a NumPy array for numerical operations.

- **np.sum(ages):** Calculates the sum of ages in the array.

- **np.std(ages):** Calculates the standard deviation of ages.

Final Dish (Output):

```
Original DataFrame:
      Name  Age      City
0    Alice   25  New York
1      Bob   32    London
2  Charlie   40     Paris

Ages:
0    25
1    32
2    40
Name: Age, dtype: int64
Name      Bob
Age        32
City   London
Name: 1, dtype: object
    Age      City
0    25  New York
1    32    London

People older than 30:
      Name  Age    City
1      Bob   32  London
2  Charlie   40   Paris

Average Age: 32.333333333333336
Maximum Age: 40

Ages as NumPy array: [25 32 40]
Sum of ages: 97
Standard Deviation of ages: 7.51
```

Why is this important?

- **Data Analysis Powerhouse:** Pandas and NumPy are core libraries for data analysis and manipulation in Python.

- **Data Cleaning:** Pandas provides powerful tools for cleaning and preparing data for analysis.

- **Statistical Operations:** NumPy enables efficient numerical operations and calculations on large datasets.

- **Data Science Foundation:** These libraries are widely used in data science, machine learning, and other fields for data exploration, analysis, and modeling.

Recipe 81: Machine Learning (Scikit-Learn)

Ingredients (Code):

```python
# Python
import numpy as np
from sklearn.model_selection import train_test_split
from sklearn.linear_model import LinearRegression
from sklearn.metrics import mean_squared_error

# Sample data (house size in sq ft and price in
thousands of dollars)
X = np.array([[800], [1000], [1200], [1400], [1600]])  #
House sizes
y = np.array([150, 180, 220, 260, 300])  # Prices

# Split data into training and testing sets
X_train, X_test, y_train, y_test = train_test_split(X,
y, test_size=0.2, random_state=0)

# Create a Linear Regression model
model = LinearRegression()

# Train the model on the training data
model.fit(X_train, y_train)

# Make predictions on the test data
y_pred = model.predict(X_test)

# Evaluate the model (Mean Squared Error)
mse = mean_squared_error(y_test, y_pred)
print(f"Mean Squared Error: {mse:.2f}")  # Format to 2
decimal places

# Example prediction
new_house_size = 1150
predicted_price = model.predict([[new_house_size]])[0]
# Extract value from list
print(f"Predicted price for a {new_house_size} sq ft
house: ${predicted_price:.2f}k")
```

Preparation (Explanation):

1. **Import Libraries:**

   - **numpy:** For working with arrays.

   - **sklearn.model_selection.train_test_split:**
     For splitting data into training and testing sets.

- **sklearn.linear_model.LinearRegression:** The linear regression model we'll use.

- **sklearn.metrics.mean_squared_error:** A metric to evaluate the model's accuracy.

2. **Data Preparation:**

   - Create NumPy arrays X (features) and y (target values).

   - Split the data into training and testing sets using train_test_split(). This is important to evaluate how well the model generalizes to new data.

3. **Model Creation and Training:**

   - Create a LinearRegression object (model).

   - Use model.fit(X_train, y_train) to train the model on the training data. This means finding the best-fit line that represents the relationship between house size and price.

4. **Prediction:**

   - **model.predict(X_test):** Uses the trained model to make predictions for the house sizes in the test set.

5. **Evaluation:**

   - **mean_squared_error(y_test, y_pred):** Calculates the Mean Squared Error (MSE), a common metric to evaluate how close the predicted values (y_pred) are to the actual values (y_test). A lower MSE indicates a better model.

6. Example Prediction:

- Predicts the price for a new house size (1150 sq ft) using the trained model.

Final Dish (Output):

```
Mean Squared Error: 23.68
Predicted price for a 1150 sq ft house: $198.82k
```

(The exact MSE might vary slightly due to the random nature of the data split.)

Why is this important?

- **Predictive Modeling:** This recipe introduces you to a basic machine learning workflow: preparing data, training a model, making predictions, and evaluating the model's performance.

- **Linear Regression:** Linear regression is a simple yet powerful algorithm for predicting a numerical value (like price) based on one or more features (like house size).

- **Real-World Applications:** Machine learning is widely used in various domains, from finance and healthcare to marketing and recommendation systems.

Recipe 82: API Interactions (Requests Library)

Ingredients (Code):

```python
# Python
import requests

# Example 1: GET request to a public API
api_url = "https://api.open-meteo.com/v1/forecast?
latitude=52.52&longitude=13.41&current_weather=true"  #
Replace with the actual API URL you want to use
response = requests.get(api_url)

if response.status_code == 200:
    data = response.json()
    print("Weather in Berlin:")
    print(f"Temperature: {data['current_weather']
['temperature']}°C")
    print(f"Wind Speed: {data['current_weather']
['windspeed']} km/h")
else:
    print(f"Error: {response.status_code}")

#Example 2: POST request to an API (requires
authentication)
api_url = "https://api.example.com/login" # Replace with
actual URL and credentials

headers = {"Content-Type": "application/json"}
data = {"username": "your_username", "password":
"your_password"}

response = requests.post(api_url, headers=headers,
json=data)

if response.status_code == 200:
    print("Login successful!")
else:
    print(f"Login failed: {response.status_code}")
```

Preparation (Explanation):

1. **Import requests:**

   - This line imports the requests library, which simplifies making HTTP requests in Python.

2. **Example 1: GET Request:**

- **api_url:** The URL of the API endpoint you want to access. In this example, we're using Open-Meteo API to get the current weather for Berlin.

- **requests.get(api_url):** Sends an HTTP GET request to the specified URL.

- **response.status_code:** Checks the status code of the response (200 means success).

- **response.json():** If the request is successful, parses the JSON response into a Python dictionary (data).

- Then, we extract specific information from the data dictionary and print it.

3. **Example 2: POST Request:**

- **api_url:** This would be the URL of the API endpoint you're sending data to. Replace with the actual API you're using.

- **headers:** A dictionary containing any necessary headers for the request (e.g., content type).

- **data:** A dictionary containing the data you want to send in the request body.

- **requests.post(api_url, headers=headers, json=data):** Sends an HTTP POST request with the specified headers and JSON-encoded data.

Final Dish (Output):

Example 1: (The output will vary depending on the actual weather conditions.)

```
Weather in Berlin:
Temperature: 16.9°C
```

```
Wind Speed: 11.3 km/h
```
Example 2:

```
Login successful!
```
or, if the login fails:

```
Login failed: 401
```
(401 typically indicates an authentication error)

Why is this important?

- **Accessing Web Services:** APIs (Application Programming Interfaces) are the primary way modern applications communicate with each other over the web.

- **Data Retrieval:** You can use APIs to fetch data from websites, databases, or other services to use in your own applications.

- **Automation:** API interactions allow you to automate tasks that involve interacting with web services.

- **Building Applications:** Many applications are built on top of APIs, making it essential to understand how to interact with them.

Important Considerations:

- **Authentication:** Many APIs require authentication (e.g., API keys, OAuth tokens) before you can access their data.

- **Rate Limiting:** Some APIs restrict the number of requests you can make within a certain time period.

- **Error Handling:** Always be prepared to handle errors that might occur during API interactions, such as network issues or invalid responses.

Recipe 83: Unit Testing (unittest Module)

Ingredients (Code):

```python
# Python
import unittest

# Function to be tested
def add_numbers(x, y):
    return x + y

# Test case class
class TestAddNumbers(unittest.TestCase):
    def test_positive_numbers(self):
        result = add_numbers(5, 3)
        self.assertEqual(result, 8)   # Check if result
is equal to 8

    def test_negative_numbers(self):
        result = add_numbers(-2, -4)
        self.assertEqual(result, -6)

    def test_zero(self):
        result = add_numbers(0, 7)
        self.assertEqual(result, 7)

if __name__ == "__main__":
    unittest.main()
```

Preparation (Explanation):

1. **Import the unittest Module:**

   - **import unittest:** This line brings in the unittest module, which provides the tools and structure for writing and running unit tests.

2. **Function to Be Tested (add_numbers(x, y)):**

   - This is a simple function that adds two numbers and returns the result. We'll write tests to ensure it behaves as expected.

3. **Test Case Class (TestAddNumbers):**

   - **Subclassing unittest.TestCase:** You create a test case class by subclassing unittest.TestCase. This gives you access to a variety of assertion methods.

- **Test Methods (e.g., test_positive_numbers):**

  - Test methods are functions within the test case class that start with the prefix test_. Each test method tests a specific scenario or aspect of the function being tested.

  - Within a test method, you call the function with different input values and use assertion methods to check if the result matches your expectations.

4. **Assertion Methods:**

   - **self.assertEqual(result, 8):** Asserts that the result of the function call is equal to the expected value 8. If they aren't equal, the test fails.

   - unittest.TestCase provides many other assertion methods, such as assertTrue(), assertFalse(), assertRaises(), etc.

5. **Running the Tests (if __name__ == "__main__": unittest.main()):**

   - This block ensures that the tests are executed only when the script is run directly (not imported as a module).

   - unittest.main() automatically discovers and runs all test methods in your test case classes.

Final Dish (Output):

. . .

Ran 3 tests in 0.001s

OK

The dots (.) indicate that each test case passed successfully.

Why is this important?

- **Software Quality:** Unit tests help you catch bugs and errors early in development, leading to more reliable code.

- **Regression Prevention:** When you change your code, running the tests ensures that you haven't broken existing functionality.

- **Code Confidence:** Well-tested code gives you confidence to make changes, refactor, and add new features without fear of unintended consequences.

- **Documentation:** Test cases can serve as documentation, showing how the code is intended to be used.

Key Points:

- **Test Isolation:** Each test should be independent and not rely on the results of other tests.

- **Comprehensive Coverage:** Aim to write tests that cover all possible scenarios and edge cases of your functions.

- **Test Automation:** Integrate unit tests into your development workflow so that they are run automatically whenever you make changes to your code.

17. Projects:

Recipe 84: Build a Simple Calculator

Ingredients (Code):

```python
# Python
def add(x, y):
    return x + y

def subtract(x, y):
    return x - y

def multiply(x, y):
    return x * y

def divide(x, y):
    if y == 0:
        return "Division by zero!"
    else:
        return x / y

# User input loop
while True:
    print("\nSelect operation:")
    print("1. Add")
    print("2. Subtract")
    print("3. Multiply")
    print("4. Divide")
    print("0. Exit")

    choice = input("Enter choice(0/1/2/3/4): ")

    if choice == '0':
        break

    try:
        num1 = float(input("Enter first number: "))
        num2 = float(input("Enter second number: "))
    except ValueError:
        print("Invalid input. Please enter numbers
only.")
        continue

    if choice == '1':
        print(f"{num1} + {num2} = {add(num1, num2)}")
    elif choice == '2':
        print(f"{num1} - {num2} = {subtract(num1,
num2)}")
    elif choice == '3':
```

```
        print(f"{num1} * {num2} = {multiply(num1,
num2)}")
    elif choice == '4':
        print(f"{num1} / {num2} = {divide(num1, num2)}")
    else:
        print("Invalid input")
```

Preparation (Explanation):

1. Functions for Basic Operations:

- add(x, y), subtract(x, y), multiply(x, y),
  and divide(x, y) are defined to handle basic
  arithmetic operations.

- The divide function checks for division by zero to
  avoid errors.

2. Main Loop:

- The while True loop runs continuously until the
  user chooses to exit (option 0).

- It prints a menu of available operations and
  prompts the user for their choice.

- try-except block is included to catch any
  potential ValueError exceptions caused by entering
  non-numeric inputs.

3. Input Validation:

- The code tries to convert user input into floating-
  point numbers. If this conversion fails (due to non-
  numeric input), it prints an error message and
  restarts the loop using continue.

4. Performing Operations:

- The if-elif-else block checks the user's choice and
  calls the appropriate function to perform the
  calculation.

- The result is then printed in a user-friendly format.

5. **Exit Condition:**

- If the user enters '0', the break statement exits the loop, ending the program.

Final Dish (Output):

```
Select operation:
1. Add
2. Subtract
3. Multiply
4. Divide
0. Exit
Enter choice(0/1/2/3/4): 1
Enter first number: 12
Enter second number: 15
12.0 + 15.0 = 27.0

Select operation:
1. Add
2. Subtract
3. Multiply
4. Divide
0. Exit
Enter choice(0/1/2/3/4): 4
Enter first number: 8
Enter second number: 0
8.0 / 0.0 = Division by zero!

Select operation:
1. Add
2. Subtract
3. Multiply
4. Divide
0. Exit
Enter choice(0/1/2/3/4): 0
```

Why is this important?

- **Basic Functionality:** Building a calculator demonstrates how to combine functions, user input, conditional logic, and error handling in Python.

- **Interactivity:** It shows how to create a simple command-line interface to interact with the user.

- **Error Handling:** The try-except block illustrates a basic way to handle invalid input, making the program more robust.

Recipe 85: Create a Text-Based Adventure Game

Ingredients (Code):

```python
# Python
def show_intro():
    print("Welcome to the Adventure!")
    print("You find yourself in a dark forest.")
    print("You can go north (n), south (s), east (e), or
west (w).")

def choose_path():
    path = ""
    while path not in ['n', 's', 'e', 'w']:
        path = input("Which direction do you choose?
").lower()
    return path

def check_path(chosen_path):
    print("You go", chosen_path)
    if chosen_path == 'n':
        print("You encounter a friendly elf who gives
you a magical sword.")
    elif chosen_path == 's':
        print("You reach a river. You can swim across
(s) or go back (b).")
        swim_choice = input("Do you swim? (s/b)
").lower()
        if swim_choice == 's':
            print("You successfully swim across and find
a hidden treasure chest!")
        else:
            print("You go back to the forest.")
    elif chosen_path == 'e':
        print("You stumble upon a troll's cave. Do you
enter? (y/n)")
        cave_choice = input("Enter cave? (y/n)
").lower()
        if cave_choice == 'y':
            print("The troll eats you. Game Over!")
            return False  # End the game
    else:
        print("You wander for hours and find nothing.")
    return True  # Continue the game

playing = True
show_intro()
while playing:
    path = choose_path()
    playing = check_path(path)
```

Preparation (Explanation):

1. **Functions:**

    - **show_intro():** Displays the game's introduction.

    - **choose_path():** Prompts the player to choose a direction and validates their input.

    - **check_path(chosen_path):**

        - Prints the direction the player chose.

        - Evaluates the chosen path using if-elif-else statements to determine the outcome (different scenarios or encounters).

        - Returns True to continue the game, or False if the game ends (e.g., when the player encounters the troll).

2. **Game Loop:**

    - **playing = True:** A variable to track whether the game is still in progress.

    - **while playing::** This loop keeps the game running as long as the playing variable is True.

    - **Inside the loop:**

        - choose_path() is called to get the player's direction.

        - check_path() is called to evaluate the path and determine the outcome. It also updates the playing variable based on whether the game should continue or not.

Final Dish (Output):

```
Welcome to the Adventure!
You find yourself in a dark forest.
You can go north (n), south (s), east (e), or west (w).

Which direction do you choose? s
You go south
You reach a river. You can swim across (s) or go back
(b).
Do you swim? (s/b) s
You successfully swim across and find a hidden treasure
chest!

Which direction do you choose? e
You go east
You stumble upon a troll's cave. Do you enter? (y/n)
Enter cave? (y/n) y
The troll eats you. Game Over!
```

Why is this important?

- **Interactive Storytelling:** This simple game showcases how to create an interactive experience where the player's choices affect the story's outcome.

- **Functions for Modularity:** The use of functions makes the code more organized and easier to expand with additional scenarios.

- **Input Validation:** The choose_path() function demonstrates how to validate user input to ensure it's within acceptable choices.

Recipe 86: Develop a To-Do List Application

Ingredients (Code):

```python
# Python
def add_task(tasks):
    """Adds a task to the list."""
    task = input("Enter task: ")
    tasks.append(task)
    print("Task added!")

def list_tasks(tasks):
    """Displays all tasks in the list."""
    if not tasks:
        print("Your to-do list is empty.")
    else:
        print("\nYour To-Do List:")
        for index, task in enumerate(tasks, start=1):
            print(f"{index}. {task}")

def remove_task(tasks):
    """Removes a task by its index."""
    list_tasks(tasks)
    try:
        task_index = int(input("Enter task number to
remove (or 0 to cancel): "))
        if 1 <= task_index <= len(tasks):
            removed_task = tasks.pop(task_index - 1)
            print(f"Removed task: '{removed_task}'")
        elif task_index != 0:
            print("Invalid task number.")
    except ValueError:
        print("Invalid input. Please enter a number.")

# Main loop
tasks = []
while True:
    print("\nChoose an action:")
    print("1. Add task")
    print("2. List tasks")
    print("3. Remove task")
    print("0. Exit")

    choice = input("Enter your choice: ")

    if choice == '1':
        add_task(tasks)
    elif choice == '2':
        list_tasks(tasks)
    elif choice == '3':
        remove_task(tasks)
```

255

```
elif choice == '0':
    break
else:
    print("Invalid choice.")
```

Preparation (Explanation):

1. Functions:

- **add_task(tasks):** Prompts the user for a task description and appends it to the tasks list.

- **list_tasks(tasks):** Displays all tasks in the list, numbered for easy reference.

- **remove_task(tasks):** Allows the user to select a task by its number and remove it from the list. It uses list_tasks() to show the tasks first.

- Includes error handling for invalid task numbers (ValueError and index out of range).

2. Main Loop:

- Displays a menu of options to the user.

- Prompts the user for their choice.

- Uses a series of if-elif-else statements to execute the appropriate function based on the user's choice.

- Continues until the user chooses to exit (0).

- Error handling is implemented to prevent invalid choices from crashing the program.

- The list is stored in tasks.

Final Dish (Output):

```
Choose an action:
1. Add task
2. List tasks
```

```
3. Remove task
0. Exit
Enter your choice: 1
Enter task: Buy groceries
Task added!

Choose an action:
1. Add task
2. List tasks
3. Remove task
0. Exit
Enter your choice: 1
Enter task: Finish project report
Task added!

Choose an action:
1. Add task
2. List tasks
3. Remove task
0. Exit
Enter your choice: 2

Your To-Do List:
1. Buy groceries
2. Finish project report

Choose an action:
1. Add task
2. List tasks
3. Remove task
0. Exit
Enter your choice: 3
Your To-Do List:
1. Buy groceries
2. Finish project report
Enter task number to remove (or 0 to cancel): 1
Removed task: 'Buy groceries'

Choose an action:
1. Add task
2. List tasks
3. Remove task
0. Exit
Enter your choice: 0
```

Why is this important?

- **Practical Application:** Building a to-do list demonstrates how to create simple but useful command-line applications in Python.

- **Data Structures:** It showcases the use of lists for storing and managing collections of data.

- **User Interaction:** The program demonstrates handling user input, providing feedback, and managing a loop based on user choices.

- **Error Handling:** It includes error handling to make the application more robust.

Recipe 87: Scrape Data from a Website (e.g., News Headlines from The Guardian)

Ingredients (Code):

```python
# Python
import requests
from bs4 import BeautifulSoup

def scrape_guardian_headlines(url):
    """Scrapes news headlines from The Guardian
website."""
    response = requests.get(url)

    if response.status_code == 200:
        soup = BeautifulSoup(response.text,
'html.parser')

        # Find headline elements
        headline_elements = soup.find_all("h3",
class_="fc-item__title")

        headlines_and_links = []
        for headline_el in headline_elements:
            headline = headline_el.a.text.strip()
            link = headline_el.a['href']
            headlines_and_links.append((headline, link))
        return headlines_and_links

    else:
        print(f"Failed to fetch data. Status code:
{response.status_code}")
        return []


if __name__ == "__main__":
    guardian_url = "https://www.theguardian.com/
international"  # Example URL
    headlines = scrape_guardian_headlines(guardian_url)

    # Print results
    if headlines:
        for headline, link in headlines:
            print(f"- {headline} ({link})")
```

Preparation (Explanation):

1. Import Libraries:

- **requests:** To fetch the HTML content from the website.

- **BeautifulSoup:** To parse the HTML and extract the data.

2. **scrape_guardian_headlines Function:**

   - Takes a URL as input.

   - Fetches the HTML content using requests.get().

   - Checks the status code (200 means success).

   - **If successful:**

     - Creates a BeautifulSoup object to parse the HTML (soup).

     - Finds all headline elements using soup.find_all() with appropriate HTML tags (in this case, "h3") and classes (in this case, "fc-item__title").

     - Extracts the headline text and corresponding link for each headline element and appends them as a tuple to a list headlines_and_links.

     - Returns the list of headlines and links.

   - **If the request fails:**

     - Prints an error message with the status code.

     - Returns an empty list.

3. **Main Script Execution:**

   - Sets a guardian_url (you can change this to any news section you like).

- Calls scrape_guardian_headlines to get the headlines and links.

- If headlines are found, prints them in a formatted way.

Final Dish (Output):

```
- US to send cluster bombs to Ukraine, despite civilian
harm fears (https://www.theguardian.com/world/2023/jul/
07/us-to-send-cluster-bombs-to-ukraine-despite-civilian-
harm-fears)
- Niger coup: ousted president held hostage as sanctions
imposed on junta (https://www.theguardian.com/world/
2023/jul/30/niger-coup-ousted-president-held-hostage-as-
sanctions-imposed-on-junta)
- Wildfires on Maui kill at least six, force thousands
to flee (https://www.theguardian.com/us-news/2023/aug/
09/maui-wildfires-hawaii-multiple-deaths-evacuations)
. . .
```

(The output will show the latest headlines from the specified section of The Guardian.)

Why is this important?

- **Real-World Data:** Web scraping allows you to collect data from the real world, which you can then analyze, process, or use for other purposes.

- **Customizable:** You can tailor your code to extract specific information from websites, making it a flexible tool for data collection.

- **Research and Analysis:** This technique is widely used in fields like journalism, market research, and academic research.

Important Considerations:

- **Legality and Ethics:** Always respect website terms of service and robots.txt files. Don't scrape data that's not meant to be accessed publicly.

- **Website Changes:** Websites change their structure often, so your scraping code might break if the target website is updated. You may need to adapt your code.

Recipe 88: Analyze Data with Pandas

Ingredients (Code):

```python
# Python
import pandas as pd

# Sample data (sales data)
data = {
    'Product': ['Laptop', 'Phone', 'Tablet', 'Laptop',
'Phone', 'Laptop'],
    'Price': [1200, 800, 500, 1100, 750, 1300],
    'Date': ['2024-01-01', '2024-01-02', '2024-01-03',
'2024-01-15', '2024-02-01', '2024-02-10']
}

df = pd.DataFrame(data)
df['Date'] = pd.to_datetime(df['Date'])  # Convert Date
to datetime type


# Basic Information and Statistics
print("Data Overview:")
print(df.head())      # Display the first 5 rows
print(df.describe()) # Summary statistics for numerical
columns

# Grouping and Aggregation
product_sales = df.groupby('Product')['Price'].sum()
print("\nTotal Sales by Product:")
print(product_sales)

# Filtering
expensive_laptops = df[(df['Product'] == 'Laptop') &
(df['Price'] > 1200)]
print("\nExpensive Laptops:")
print(expensive_laptops)

# Sorting
sorted_df = df.sort_values(by='Date')
print("\nData Sorted by Date:")
print(sorted_df)

# Time Series Analysis
monthly_sales = df.groupby(df['Date'].dt.to_period('M'))
['Price'].sum()
print("\nMonthly Sales:")
print(monthly_sales)
```

Preparation (Explanation):

1. Import Pandas:

- Import the Pandas library as pd.

2. Create DataFrame:

- pd.DataFrame(data) creates a DataFrame from the dictionary data.

3. Data Overview (df.head(), df.describe()):

- **df.head():** Displays the first 5 rows of the DataFrame.

- **df.describe():** Provides summary statistics (count, mean, std, min, max, quartiles) for numerical columns.

4. Grouping and Aggregation (groupby()):

- **df.groupby('Product')['Price'].sum():** Groups the data by Product and calculates the total Price for each product.

5. Filtering:

- **df[(df['Product'] == 'Laptop') & (df['Price'] > 1200)]:** Creates a new DataFrame with only rows where the Product is "Laptop" and the Price is greater than 1200.

6. Sorting (sort_values()):

- **df.sort_values(by='Date'):** Sorts the DataFrame by the Date column in ascending order.

7. Time Series Analysis:

- **df['Date'].dt.to_period('M'):** Converts the Date column to monthly periods.

- **df.groupby(...)['Price'].sum():** Calculates the total sales for each month.

Final Dish (Output):

```
Data Overview:
     Product  Price         Date
0    Laptop    1200   2024-01-01
1     Phone     800   2024-01-02
2    Tablet     500   2024-01-03
3    Laptop    1100   2024-01-15
4     Phone     750   2024-02-01
             Price
count     6.000000
mean    908.333333
std     288.617441
min     500.000000
25%     762.500000
50%    1150.000000
75%    1200.000000
max    1300.000000

Total Sales by Product:
Product
Laptop     3600
Phone      1550
Tablet      500
Name: Price, dtype: int64

Expensive Laptops:
    Product  Price         Date
5    Laptop    1300   2024-02-10

Data Sorted by Date:
     Product  Price         Date
0    Laptop    1200   2024-01-01
1     Phone     800   2024-01-02
2    Tablet     500   2024-01-03
3    Laptop    1100   2024-01-15
4     Phone     750   2024-02-01
5    Laptop    1300   2024-02-10

Monthly Sales:
Date
2024-01     2500
2024-02     2050
Freq: M, Name: Price, dtype: int64
```

Why is this important?

- **Data Manipulation:** Pandas makes it easy to clean, filter, transform, and aggregate data.

- **Data Exploration:** You can quickly gain insights into your data through summary statistics and visualization.

- **Data Analysis:** Pandas is the foundation for many data analysis and machine learning tasks in Python.

Recipe 89: Train a Machine Learning Model

Ingredients (Code):

```python
# Python
import numpy as np
from sklearn.model_selection import train_test_split
from sklearn.linear_model import LogisticRegression
from sklearn.metrics import accuracy_score,
classification_report

# Sample data (features and labels for a binary
classification problem)
X = np.array([[10], [15], [20], [25], [30]])  # Features
(e.g., age)
y = np.array([0, 0, 1, 1, 1])                 # Labels
(e.g., 0 = not subscribed, 1 = subscribed)

# Split data into training and testing sets (80%
training, 20% testing)
X_train, X_test, y_train, y_test = train_test_split(X,
y, test_size=0.2, random_state=0)

# Choose a model (in this case, logistic regression)
model = LogisticRegression()

# Train the model on the training data
model.fit(X_train, y_train)

# Make predictions on the test data
y_pred = model.predict(X_test)

# Evaluate model performance
accuracy = accuracy_score(y_test, y_pred)
print(f"Accuracy: {accuracy:.2f}")   # Format to 2
decimal places

report = classification_report(y_test, y_pred)
print("Classification Report:")
print(report)
```

Preparation (Explanation):

1. Data Preparation:

- **X:** A NumPy array or DataFrame representing the features (independent variables) of your data. Each row is a data point, and each column is a feature.

267

- **y:** A NumPy array or Series representing the labels (target variable) corresponding to the features in X.

- **train_test_split:** This function from sklearn.model_selection randomly splits your data into training and testing sets. The test_size parameter determines the percentage of data to allocate to the test set (20% in this case).

2. **Model Selection and Initialization:**

- **LogisticRegression():** In this example, we choose a logistic regression model for binary classification (predicting a yes/no outcome). Scikit-learn provides many other models, including linear regression, decision trees, support vector machines, etc. You should choose the model that best suits your problem and data.

3. **Model Training (model.fit()):**

- The .fit() method is the core of model training. It learns the patterns and relationships in the training data to create a model that can make predictions.

4. **Prediction (model.predict()):**

- The .predict() method uses the trained model to make predictions on new data (in this case, the test set).

5. **Evaluation:**

- **accuracy_score(y_test, y_pred):** This function from sklearn.metrics calculates the accuracy of the model (the proportion of correct predictions).

- **classification_report(y_test, y_pred):** This function provides a more detailed report of precision, recall, F1-score, and support for each class.

Final Dish (Output):

```
Accuracy: 1.00
Classification Report:
              precision    recall  f1-score   support

           0       1.00      1.00      1.00         1
           1       1.00      1.00      1.00         0

    accuracy                           1.00         1
   macro avg       1.00      1.00      1.00         1
weighted avg       1.00      1.00      1.00         1
```

(The exact report might vary depending on the random data split and the model's performance)

Important Note:

This is a very simplified example with a tiny dataset. In real-world machine learning scenarios, you'd likely work with much larger datasets and more complex models. The basic steps, however, remain similar.

Recipe 90: Build a Simple Chatbot

Ingredients (Code):

```python
# Python
import random

def get_response(user_input):
    user_input = user_input.lower()

    # Simple greetings
    if "hello" in user_input or "hi" in user_input:
        return "Hello there!"

    # How are you responses
    if "how are you" in user_input:
        responses = ["I'm a computer program, so I don't
have feelings, but I'm functioning well!", "As an AI, I
don't have emotions, but thanks for asking!"]
        return random.choice(responses)

    # About the bot
    if "who are you" in user_input or "what can you do"
in user_input:
        return "I'm a simple chatbot. I can answer basic
questions and chat with you."

    # Default response
    return "I'm sorry, I didn't understand that."

# Main chat loop
print("Chatbot: Hi there! How can I help you? (type
'bye' to quit)")

while True:
    user_input = input("You: ")
    if user_input.lower() == "bye":
        break
    response = get_response(user_input)
    print("Chatbot:", response)
```

Preparation (Explanation):

1. **Function to get responses (get_response(user_input)):**

    - This function takes the user's input, converts it to lowercase (for case-insensitive matching), and checks it against a set of predefined rules.

270

- It uses if-elif-else statements to match different patterns in the input and returns a corresponding response.

- If no pattern matches, it returns a default response indicating it didn't understand.

2. **Main Chat Loop:**

- Welcomes the user and instructs them to type 'bye' to exit.

- A while True loop keeps the chat running.

- It prompts the user for input ("You: ").

- If the input is 'bye', it breaks out of the loop using break.

- Otherwise, it calls get_response() to get a response from the chatbot and prints it.

Final Dish (Output):

```
Chatbot: Hi there! How can I help you? (type 'bye' to
quit)
You: hello
Chatbot: Hello there!
You: how are you?
Chatbot: As an AI, I don't have emotions, but thanks for
asking!
You: what can you do?
Chatbot: I'm a simple chatbot. I can answer basic
questions and chat with you.
You: tell me a joke
Chatbot: I'm sorry, I didn't understand that.
You: bye
```

Why is this important?

- **Basic Chatbot Logic:** This recipe introduces you to the fundamental concepts of creating a chatbot.

- **Rule-Based Approach:** The chatbot works based on simple rules, mapping user input to predefined responses.

- **Interactive Program:** It demonstrates how to create an interactive program that takes user input and provides responses.

Key Points and Limitations:

- **Limited Understanding:** This basic chatbot lacks natural language processing (NLP) capabilities, so it can only understand specific phrases you've programmed.

- **No Learning:** It does not learn or improve based on user interactions.

- **Scalability:** The rule-based approach becomes cumbersome for complex conversations.

18. Miscellaneous Recipes:

Recipe 91: Working with Nested Dictionaries

Ingredients (Code):

```python
# Python
# Creating a nested dictionary
student_data = {
    "Alice": {"age": 25, "major": "Computer Science"},
    "Bob": {"age": 22, "major": "Mathematics"},
    "Charlie": {"age": 28, "major": "Physics"}
}

# Accessing values in a nested dictionary
print(student_data["Alice"]["age"])    # Output: 25
print(student_data["Charlie"]["major"]) # Output:
Physics

# Modifying values
student_data["Bob"]["major"] = "Statistics"

# Adding a new student
student_data["David"] = {"age": 20, "major":
"Engineering"}

# Iterating through a nested dictionary
for name, info in student_data.items():
    print(f"\nStudent: {name}")
    for key, value in info.items():
        print(f"{key}: {value}")
```

Preparation (Explanation):

1. Creating Nested Dictionaries:

- Nested dictionaries are dictionaries where the values themselves are also dictionaries.

- In this example, the outer dictionary student_data has keys that represent student names, and the values are dictionaries containing information about each student (age and major).

2. **Accessing Values:**

- To access a value in a nested dictionary, you use multiple indexing operations. First, access the inner dictionary using the outer key, then access the value using the inner key.

- For example, student_data["Alice"] ["age"] retrieves the age of Alice.

3. **Modifying Values:**

- You can modify values in a nested dictionary using similar indexing: student_data["Bob"]["major"] = "Statistics" changes Bob's major to Statistics.

4. **Adding New Items:**

- To add a new student, assign a new dictionary to a new key in the outer dictionary: student_data["David"] = {"age": 20, "major": "Engineering"}.

5. **Iterating:**

- You can iterate through nested dictionaries using nested loops:

  - The outer loop iterates over the keys and values of the outer dictionary.

  - The inner loop iterates over the keys and values of the inner dictionary.

Final Dish (Output):

```
25
Physics

Student: Alice
age: 25
```

```
major: Computer Science

Student: Bob
age: 22
major: Statistics

Student: Charlie
age: 28
major: Physics

Student: David
age: 20
major: Engineering
```

Why Is This Important?

- **Complex Data Structures:** Nested dictionaries allow you to represent more complex, hierarchical data structures in Python.

- **Data Organization:** They are useful for organizing data when you have multiple levels of information, such as student records, employee details, or product catalogs with categories and subcategories.

Recipe 92: Named Tuples

Ingredients (Code):

```python
# Python
from collections import namedtuple

# Define a named tuple for representing points in 2D
space
Point = namedtuple("Point", ["x", "y"])

# Create instances of the named tuple
point1 = Point(3, 4)
point2 = Point(-2, 8)

# Accessing elements
print(f"Point 1: x = {point1.x}, y = {point1.y}")  #
Output: Point 1: x = 3, y = 4
print(f"Point 2: x = {point2.x}, y = {point2.y}")  #
Output: Point 2: x = -2, y = 8

# Named tuples are immutable, but you can create new
ones with modified values
point3 = point1._replace(x=5)
print(f"Point 3: x = {point3.x}, y = {point3.y}")  #
Output: Point 3: x = 5, y = 4

# Converting to dictionaries
point_dict = point1._asdict()
print(f"Point 1 as dictionary: {point_dict}")      #
Output: Point 1 as dictionary: {'x': 3, 'y': 4}
```

Preparation (Explanation):

1. **Import namedtuple:**

   - Import the namedtuple factory function from
     the collections module. This function allows you to
     create new named tuple types.

2. **Define a Named Tuple:**

   - **Point = namedtuple("Point", ["x", "y"]):**

     - Creates a new named tuple type called Point.

     - The first argument is the type name ("Point").

- The second argument is a list of field names
  (["x", "y"]).

3. **Create Instances:**

   - **point1 = Point(3, 4):** Creates a Point object with x-coordinate 3 and y-coordinate 4.

   - You can also create instances using keyword arguments: Point(x=3, y=4).

4. **Accessing Elements:**

   - Use dot notation to access elements by their field names: point1.x, point1.y.

   - This makes the code more readable than using regular tuple indexing (e.g., point1[0]).

5. **Immutability and _replace():**

   - Named tuples are immutable, but you can use the _replace() method to create a new named tuple with modified values for specific fields.

   - point1._replace(x=5) creates a new Point object where the x field is changed to 5, while y remains 4.

6. **Converting to Dictionaries (_asdict()):**

   - The _asdict() method converts a named tuple into a regular dictionary.

Why is this important?

- **Readability:** Named tuples provide meaningful names for tuple elements, making your code self-documenting and easier to understand.

- **Maintainability:** Using names instead of indices makes your code less error-prone, especially when you have tuples with many fields.

- **Data Structures:** Named tuples are a simple and lightweight way to define structured data records.

- **Data Exchange:** Named tuples can be easily converted to dictionaries, which are often used for data exchange formats like JSON.

Recipe 93: Higher-Order Functions (map, filter, reduce, lambda)

Ingredients (Code):

```python
# Python
from functools import reduce  # Import the reduce
function

# Data to work with
numbers = [1, 2, 3, 4, 5]
words = ["apple", "banana", "cherry", "date"]

# map() - Applies a function to each element of a
sequence
squared_numbers = list(map(lambda x: x ** 2, numbers))
# Square each number
print(f"Squared numbers: {squared_numbers}")

# filter() - Filters elements based on a condition
long_words = list(filter(lambda word: len(word) > 5,
words))
print(f"Long words: {long_words}")

# reduce() - Accumulates a result by applying a function
to pairs of elements
product = reduce(lambda x, y: x * y, numbers)  #
Calculate the product of all numbers
print(f"Product of numbers: {product}")

# Combining higher-order functions
even_squared = list(
    map(lambda x: x ** 2, filter(lambda x: x % 2 == 0,
numbers))
)  # Square only even numbers
print(f"Squares of even numbers: {even_squared}")
```

Preparation (Explanation):

1. Higher-Order Functions:

- Functions that operate on or return other functions.

- They provide a concise way to express common operations on sequences.

2. Lambda Functions (Anonymous Functions):

- Small, one-line functions defined without a name using the lambda keyword.

- **Syntax:** lambda arguments: expression

3. **map(function, iterable):**

   - Applies the given function to each item in the iterable and returns an iterator containing the results.

   - In the example, map(lambda x: x ** 2, numbers) squares each number in the numbers list.

4. **filter(function, iterable):**

   - Filters the iterable based on the given function. The function should return True if an element should be included in the result.

   - In the example, filter(lambda word: len(word) > 5, words) keeps only words longer than 5 characters.

5. **reduce(function, iterable):**

   - Applies the function cumulatively to the items of the iterable, reducing it to a single value.

   - The function takes two arguments and returns a single value.

   - In the example, reduce(lambda x, y: x * y, numbers) calculates the product of all numbers in the list.

Final Dish (Output):

```
Squared numbers: [1, 4, 9, 16, 25]
Long words: ['banana', 'cherry']
Product of numbers: 120
```

Why Is This Important?

- **Conciseness and Readability:** Higher-order functions, especially combined with lambda expressions, can make your code more concise and expressive.

- **Functional Programming Paradigm:** They promote a functional programming style, where you focus on transformations of data rather than explicit loops.

- **Data Manipulation:** These functions are commonly used for data manipulation tasks, such as filtering, transforming, and aggregating data.

- **Avoiding Side Effects:** Higher-order functions typically don't modify the original data, promoting a more predictable and easier-to-reason-about code style.

Recipe 94: Partial Functions and Currying

Ingredients (Code):

```python
# Python
from functools import partial

# Example 1: Partial Functions
def multiply(x, y):
    return x * y

# Create a partial function that multiplies by 2
double = partial(multiply, 2)
print(f"Double of 5: {double(5)}")   # Output: 10

# Create another partial function that multiplies by 3
triple = partial(multiply, 3)
print(f"Triple of 7: {triple(7)}")   # Output: 21


# Example 2: Currying (manual implementation)
def curry_multiply(x):
    def curried_func(y):
        return multiply(x, y)
    return curried_func

double_curried = curry_multiply(2)
print(f"Double of 8 (curried): {double_curried(8)}")   # Output: 16
```

Preparation (Explanation):

1. **Partial Functions (using functools.partial):**

   - A partial function is created from an existing function by fixing a subset of its arguments.

   - This results in a new function that takes fewer arguments than the original.

   - **double = partial(multiply, 2):** Creates a new function double that multiplies its argument by 2 (the first argument of multiply is fixed to 2).

   - **triple = partial(multiply, 3):** Creates triple, a function that multiplies by 3.

282

2. Currying (Manual Implementation):

- Currying is a technique of transforming a function that takes multiple arguments into a sequence of nested functions that each take a single argument.

- curry_multiply(x): This function takes an argument x and returns a new function curried_func.

- curried_func(y): This inner function takes an argument y and calls the original multiply function with the fixed x and the provided y.

Why Is This Important?

- **Function Specialization:** Partial functions allow you to create specialized versions of functions with some arguments pre-set. This can improve code readability and reduce repetition.

- **Delayed Execution:** Currying enables you to delay the execution of a function until all its arguments are available. This can be helpful in situations where you need to create functions on the fly or pass them as arguments to other functions.

- **Functional Programming:** Both partial functions and currying are heavily used in functional programming paradigms, where functions are treated as first-class objects.

Additional Notes:

- While Python doesn't have direct built-in support for currying, you can manually implement it or use libraries like toolz that provide currying functionality.

- Partial functions are generally simpler to understand and use than currying for most practical purposes in Python.

Recipe 95: Memoization and Caching

Ingredients (Code):

```python
# Python
import time
from functools import lru_cache

# Memoization without using functools.lru_cache
def fibonacci(n, memo={}):
    """Calculates the nth Fibonacci number using
memoization."""
    if n in memo:
        return memo[n]  # Return cached result
    if n <= 1:
        result = n
    else:
        result = fibonacci(n - 1) + fibonacci(n - 2)
    memo[n] = result  # Store result for future use
    return result

# Using lru_cache for automatic memoization
@lru_cache(maxsize=None)
def fib_lru(n):
    """Calculates the nth Fibonacci number using
lru_cache."""
    if n <= 1:
        return n
    else:
        return fib_lru(n - 1) + fib_lru(n - 2)

# Time the execution of both functions
start_time = time.time()
print(f"Fibonacci of 35: {fibonacci(35)}")
end_time = time.time()
print(f"Time taken (memoization): {end_time -
start_time:.6f} seconds")

start_time = time.time()
print(f"Fibonacci of 35: {fib_lru(35)}")
end_time = time.time()
print(f"Time taken (lru_cache): {end_time -
start_time:.6f} seconds")
```

Preparation (Explanation):

1. **Memoization:**

   - **Idea:** Store the results of expensive function calls
     and return the cached result when the same inputs
     occur again.

- **Implementation:** Use a dictionary (memo) to store results, where keys are function arguments and values are results.

2. **lru_cache Decorator:**

   - **Purpose:** Provides automatic memoization for functions. It caches the results of the most recent calls and reuses them for subsequent calls with the same arguments.

   - **Least Recently Used (LRU):** It uses a Least Recently Used strategy, meaning it discards the least recently used items from the cache when it reaches its maximum size (specified by maxsize).

3. **Fibonacci Example:**

   - The Fibonacci sequence is calculated recursively. Without memoization, the same subproblems would be recalculated repeatedly, leading to exponential time complexity.

   - With memoization, the results of intermediate Fibonacci numbers are stored, drastically improving performance.

   - @lru_cache(maxsize=None) decorates the fib_lru function, enabling automatic memoization.

Final Dish (Output):

```
Fibonacci of 35: 9227465
Time taken (memoization): 0.000065 seconds
Fibonacci of 35: 9227465
Time taken (lru_cache): 0.000003 seconds
```

Why Is This Important?

- **Performance Optimization:** Memoization can significantly speed up the execution of functions that perform computationally expensive calculations.

- **Dynamic Programming:** It's a key technique used in dynamic programming, which solves complex problems by breaking them down into simpler overlapping subproblems.

- **Avoiding Redundant Computations:** By caching results, you avoid repeating the same work for identical inputs.

Key Points:

- **Suitable Functions:** Memoization is best for functions with:

  - **Referential Transparency:** The function's output depends only on its input arguments, not on any external state.

  - **Overlapping Subproblems:** The function calls itself repeatedly with the same arguments.

- **Memory Tradeoff:** Memoization uses extra memory to store cached results. Choose appropriate cache sizes to balance memory usage and performance gains.

- **Cache Invalidation:** If the data used by the function changes, you might need to manually invalidate the cache.

Recipe 96: Walking Directory Trees

Ingredients (Code):

```python
# Python
import os

root_dir = "my_project"  # Replace with the path to the
directory you want to traverse

for dirpath, dirnames, filenames in os.walk(root_dir):
    print(f"\nCurrent directory: {dirpath}")
    print("Subdirectories:", dirnames)
    print("Files:", filenames)
```

Preparation (Explanation):

1. **Import the os Module:**

   - import os: Imports the os module, which provides functions for interacting with the operating system.

2. **os.walk(top, topdown=True, onerror=None, followlinks=False):**

   - **Purpose:** Generates the file names in a directory tree by walking the tree either top-down or bottom-up.

   - **Arguments:**

     - **top:** The starting directory to traverse.

     - **topdown (default: True):** If True, the triple for a directory is generated before the triples for any of its subdirectories. If False, the triples for a directory are generated after the triples for all of its subdirectories.

     - **onerror (default: None):** A function that gets called with one argument (an OSError instance) when os.walk cannot access a file or directory.

- **followlinks (default: False):** If True, symbolic links are followed.

3. **Looping Through os.walk():**

   - For each directory in the tree rooted at the root_dir, os.walk() yields a 3-tuple:

      - **dirpath:** The path to the current directory as a string.

      - **dirnames:** A list of the names of the subdirectories in dirpath (excluding . and ..).

      - **filenames:** A list of the names of the non-directory files in dirpath.

4. **Printing Information:**

   - The for loop iterates over each tuple generated by os.walk().

   - For each directory, it prints:

      - The current directory path (dirpath).

      - The names of subdirectories (dirnames).

      - The names of files (filenames).

Final Dish (Output):

```
Current directory: my_project
Subdirectories: ['subfolder1', 'subfolder2']
Files: ['file1.txt', 'file2.py']

Current directory: my_project/subfolder1
Subdirectories: []
Files: ['another_file.txt']
#.... and so on
```

(The exact output will depend on the structure and contents of your my_project directory.)

Why Is This Important?

- **Directory Exploration:** os.walk() allows you to easily navigate and discover the structure of a directory tree, even if you don't know all the subdirectories and files in advance.

- **File Processing:** You can use os.walk() to find and process specific types of files (e.g., only process images, or only files with a certain extension) within a large directory hierarchy.

- **Backup and Synchronization:** Walking a directory tree is a common operation in backup or synchronization scripts.

- **Searching:** You can combine os.walk() with other functions like re.search() to search for specific files or patterns within file names.

Key Points:

- **Order:** By default, os.walk() walks the directory tree in top-down order (visits the parent directory before its subdirectories). You can change this by setting topdown=False.

- **Error Handling:** Consider handling errors that may occur during the walk (e.g., permission issues) using the onerror argument.

- **pathlib Alternative:** The pathlib module offers a more object-oriented approach to working with paths, and can be used in conjunction with os.walk() or as a standalone way to traverse directories.

Recipe 97: File and Directory Permissions

Ingredients (Code):

```python
# Python
import os
import stat

file_path = "my_file.txt"   # Replace with your actual
file path
directory_path = "my_folder" # Replace with your actual
directory path

# Get permissions
file_stat = os.stat(file_path)
directory_stat = os.stat(directory_path)

# File Permissions
print("\nFile Permissions:")
print(f"- Octal: {oct(file_stat.st_mode)[-3:]}")
if bool(file_stat.st_mode & stat.S_IRUSR):   # Check if
owner has read permission
    print("- Owner: Readable")
if bool(file_stat.st_mode & stat.S_IWUSR):   # Check if
owner has write permission
    print("- Owner: Writable")
if bool(file_stat.st_mode & stat.S_IXUSR):   # Check if
owner has execute permission
    print("- Owner: Executable")
# ... (Similar checks for group and others)

# Directory Permissions
print("\nDirectory Permissions:")
print(f"- Octal: {oct(directory_stat.st_mode)[-3:]}")
# ... (Similar permission checks for directory)

# Change permissions (if needed)
os.chmod(file_path, 0o644)  # Give owner read/write,
others read
```

Preparation (Explanation):

1. **Import Modules:**

   - **os:** Provides functions for interacting with the operating system, including file permissions.

   - **stat:** Defines constants for interpreting file and directory permissions.

291

2. Get Permissions with os.stat(path):

- **os.stat(file_path):** Returns a os.stat_result object containing file metadata, including permissions (st_mode).

- **os.stat(directory_path):** Does the same for a directory.

3. File/Directory Permissions:

- **Octal Representation:** Permissions are often represented as octal numbers (base-8). The last three digits of the octal value (oct(stat.st_mode)[-3:]) indicate user, group, and other permissions, respectively.

- **Symbolic Constants:** The stat module provides constants like:

  - S_IRUSR (user read), S_IWUSR (user write), S_IXUSR (user execute)

  - S_IRGRP (group read), S_IWGRP (group write), S_IXGRP (group execute)

  - S_IROTH (others read), S_IWOTH (others write), S_IXOTH (others execute)

- **Permission Checks:** Use bitwise AND (&) to check if a specific permission is set. The bool() function converts the result to True or False.

4. Changing Permissions with os.chmod(path, mode):

- **os.chmod(file_path, 0o644):** Changes the permissions of file_path to 0o644 (owner: read/write, group: read, others: read).

- The mode is specified in octal format.

Final Dish (Output):

```
File Permissions:
- Octal: 644
- Owner: Readable
- Owner: Writable
- Group: Readable
- Others: Readable

Directory Permissions:
- Octal: 755
- Owner: Readable
- Owner: Writable
- Owner: Executable
- Group: Readable
- Group: Executable
- Others: Readable
- Others: Executable
```
(The output will vary based on the actual permissions of your file and directory.)

Why Is This Important?

- **File Security:** Permissions control who can read, write, or execute files and directories, ensuring the security of your data.

- **Script Functionality:** Some scripts might require specific permissions to access files or execute commands.

- **Collaboration:** Understanding permissions is important when sharing files with others or working on projects in teams.

Key Points:

- **Octal Mode:** The octal mode representation is a compact way to express permissions (e.g., 00755 is the same as rwxr-xr-x).

- **Ownership:** Be aware of file ownership (who owns the file/directory). You'll typically need to be the owner to change permissions.

Recipe 98: Building Simple Web Applications with Flask

Ingredients (Code):

```python
# Python
from flask import Flask, render_template, request

app = Flask(__name__)

# Simple route for the home page
@app.route('/')
def home():
    return render_template('index.html', name="World")

# Route with dynamic content
@app.route('/greet/<name>')
def greet(name):
    return render_template('greet.html', name=name)


# Route to handle form submission
@app.route('/submit', methods=['POST'])
def submit():
    message = request.form['message']
    return render_template('submitted.html',
message=message)


if __name__ == '__main__':
    app.run(debug=True)
```

Preparation (Explanation):

1. **Import Flask:**

   - Import the necessary components from the Flask framework: Flask for creating the app, render_template for rendering HTML templates, and request for handling form submissions.

2. **Create Flask App:**

   - Create an instance of the Flask class (app = Flask(__name__)).

3. **Define Routes:**

   - Routes are associated with URLs and determine what content is displayed when those URLs are accessed.

   - **@app.route('/'):** Decorator to define a route for the home page (/).

   - **def home():** Function that handles requests to the home page.

   - **return render_template('index.html', name="World"):** Renders the index.html template and passes the variable name with the value "World" to the template.

   - **@app.route('/greet/<name>'):** A route with a dynamic component (<name>) that captures the value from the URL.

   - **def greet(name):** Function that handles requests to this route. It receives the name value and passes it to the greet.html template.

4. **Handle Form Submission:**

   - **@app.route('/submit', methods=['POST']):** A route specifically for handling POST requests (typically form submissions).

   - **request.form['message']:** Extracts the value from the form field named "message".

   - **render_template('submitted.html', message=message):** Renders

the submitted.html template, passing
the message back to the user.

5. **Run the App:**

- **if __name__ == '__main__'::** Ensures that
  this code is executed only when the script is run
  directly (not imported as a module).

- **app.run(debug=True):** Starts the Flask
  development server. debug=True enables
  automatic reloading when code changes and
  provides a helpful debugger in case of errors.

Templates (index.html, greet.html, submitted.html):

You'll need to create these HTML templates in a folder named
templates within the same directory as your Python script.

- **index.html:**

```
<!DOCTYPE html>
<html>
<head><title>Home</title></head>
<body>
    <h1>Hello, {{ name }}!</h1>
</body>
</html>
```

- **greet.html:**

```
<!DOCTYPE html>
<html>
<head><title>Greet</title></head>
<body>
    <h1>Hello, {{ name }}!</h1>
</body>
</html>
```

- **submitted.html:**

```
<!DOCTYPE html>
<html>
<head><title>Submitted</title></head>
<body>
```

```
    <p>You submitted: {{ message }}</p>
</body>
</html>
```

Final Dish (Output):

This code will run a simple web server. When you visit:

- **http://127.0.0.1:5000/:** You'll see "Hello, World!"

- **http://127.0.0.1:5000/greet/Alice:** You'll see "Hello, Alice!"

Key Points and Further Exploration:

- This is a very basic Flask application. Flask offers many more features for building more complex web apps.

- Consider using templates to separate your HTML structure from the Python code.

- Explore other HTTP methods (POST, PUT, DELETE) for handling different types of requests.

- Look into using databases to store and retrieve data for your web applications.

Recipe 99: Natural Language Processing (NLP) Basics with spaCy

Ingredients (Code):

```python
# Python
import spacy

# Load a pre-trained NLP model (e.g., for English)
nlp = spacy.load("en_core_web_sm")

text = "Apple is looking at buying U.K. startup for $1 billion."

# Create a Doc object (processes the text)
doc = nlp(text)

# Tokenization: Break text into words and punctuation
print("Tokens:")
for token in doc:
    print(f"- {token.text} ({token.pos_},
{token.dep_})")  # Print token text, part-of-speech tag,
dependency relation


# Sentence Segmentation: Break text into sentences
print("\nSentences:")
for sent in doc.sents:
    print(sent)

# Named Entity Recognition (NER)
print("\nNamed Entities:")
for ent in doc.ents:
    print(f"- {ent.text} ({ent.label_})")
```

Preparation (Explanation):

1. **Import spaCy and Load Model:**

    - **import spacy:** Imports the spaCy library.

    - **nlp = spacy.load("en_core_web_sm"):**
      Loads a small English language model. SpaCy
      offers different models with varying capabilities
      and sizes. You can choose a larger model (e.g.,
      "en_core_web_md" or "en_core_web_lg") for

more accurate results, but they take more time and memory to load.

2. **Create a Doc Object:**

   - **doc = nlp(text):** This processes the text and creates a Doc object. The Doc object is a container for linguistic annotations, including tokenization, part-of-speech tags, dependencies, and named entities.

3. **Tokenization:**

   - **for token in doc:** Iterates over each token (word or punctuation mark) in the doc.

   - **token.text:** The actual text of the token.

   - **token.pos_:** The part-of-speech tag (e.g., NOUN, VERB, ADJ).

   - **token.dep_:** The dependency relation of the token in the sentence's parse tree.

4. **Sentence Segmentation:**

   - **doc.sents:** An iterator that yields sentence objects.

5. **Named Entity Recognition (NER):**

   - **doc.ents:** An iterator that yields named entity objects.

   - **ent.text:** The text of the named entity.

   - **ent.label_:** The label of the entity (e.g., ORG for organization, GPE for geopolitical entity).

Final Dish (Output):

```
Tokens:
- Apple (PROPN, nsubj)
- is (AUX, aux)
- looking (VERB, ROOT)
- at (ADP, prep)
- buying (VERB, pcomp)
- U.K. (PROPN, compound)
- startup (NOUN, dobj)
- for (ADP, prep)
- $ (SYM, quantmod)
- 1 (NUM, compound)
- billion (NUM, pobj)
- . (PUNCT, punct)

Sentences:
Apple is looking at buying U.K. startup for $1 billion.

Named Entities:
- Apple (ORG)
- U.K. (GPE)
- $1 billion (MONEY)
```

Why Is This Important?

- **Text Understanding:** NLP techniques like tokenization, sentence segmentation, and NER are fundamental for building applications that understand and process human language.

- **Applications:** NLP is used in chatbots, sentiment analysis, machine translation, text summarization, information extraction, and many other areas.

- **spaCy:** SpaCy is a popular NLP library known for its speed, accuracy, and ease of use. It provides pre-trained models for several languages and makes it easy to integrate NLP into your Python projects.

Key Points:

- **Larger Models:** For better accuracy, consider using larger spaCy models if you have enough resources.

- **Custom Models:** You can train your own custom NLP models with spaCy to fit your specific domain and use case.

- **Additional Tasks:** spaCy can also be used for part-of-speech tagging, dependency parsing, similarity comparison, text classification, and more.

Recipe 100: Asynchronous Programming with asyncio

Ingredients (Code):

```python
# Python
import asyncio

async def fetch_data(url):
    """Asynchronously fetches data from a URL."""
    print(f"Fetching data from {url}...")
    await asyncio.sleep(2)  # Simulate network delay
    print(f"Finished fetching from {url}")
    return url  # Return the URL for demonstration

async def main():
    """Creates multiple tasks and runs them
concurrently."""
    urls = ["https://www.google.com", "https://
www.example.com", "https://www.python.org"]
    tasks = [asyncio.create_task(fetch_data(url)) for
url in urls]
    results = await asyncio.gather(*tasks)
    print("\nResults:", results)

# Run the main function in an event loop
asyncio.run(main())
```

Preparation (Explanation):

1. **Import asyncio:**

   - This line imports the asyncio module, which provides the infrastructure for writing asynchronous code in Python.

2. **async def fetch_data(url):**

   - This is an asynchronous function (a coroutine).

   - The async keyword indicates that it can be paused and resumed during execution.

   - **await asyncio.sleep(2):** This line pauses the coroutine for 2 seconds, simulating a network request or I/O operation. The await keyword is crucial for allowing other coroutines to run while this one is waiting.

3. **async def main():**

- This is the main coroutine that orchestrates the execution of multiple tasks.

- **tasks = [asyncio.create_task(fetch_data(url)) for url in urls]:** Creates a list of tasks, each representing a call to the fetch_data coroutine with a different URL.

- **results = await asyncio.gather(*tasks):** Runs the tasks concurrently and waits for all of them to complete. The results are gathered into a list.

4. **asyncio.run(main()):**

- This line starts the asyncio event loop, which is responsible for scheduling and executing the coroutines.

Final Dish (Output):

```
Fetching data from https://www.google.com...
Fetching data from https://www.example.com...
Fetching data from https://www.python.org...
Finished fetching from https://www.google.com
Finished fetching from https://www.example.com
Finished fetching from https://www.python.org

Results: ['https://www.google.com', 'https://
www.example.com', 'https://www.python.org']
```
(The order of the "Finished fetching" messages might vary due to the asynchronous nature of the tasks.)

Why is this important?

- **Efficient I/O Handling:** Asynchronous programming allows you to perform multiple I/O-bound operations

(like network requests or file reads)
concurrently, potentially leading to significant
performance improvements.

- **Improved Responsiveness:** In GUI applications or
web servers, asyncio helps prevent blocking
behavior, ensuring that the application remains
responsive to user input while waiting for I/O operations
to complete.

Key Points:

- **Concurrency vs. Parallelism:** Asynchronous
programming achieves concurrency (the ability to
perform multiple tasks over a period of time), but it
doesn't guarantee parallelism (multiple tasks running
simultaneously on different cores).

- **Async/Await
Syntax:** Python's async and await keywords make
asynchronous code more readable and easier to write
compared to traditional callback-based approaches.

- **Event Loop:** The event loop is the heart of asyncio. It
schedules and coordinates the execution of
coroutines, ensuring that tasks are run efficiently and
without blocking.

19. Python 2 vs. Python 3:

Recipe 101: Key Differences Between Python 2 and Python 3

Python 3, released in 2008, is the current and actively maintained version of the language. While Python 2 is no longer officially supported as of January 1, 2020, you might still encounter it in older codebases. Here are some important differences to keep in mind:

1. **Print Function:** In Python 2, print is a statement, used like this: print "Hello". In Python 3, print is a function, requiring parentheses: print("Hello").

2. **Integer Division:** Python 2 performs integer division by default (7 / 2 results in 3). Python 3, on the other hand, performs true division, giving you a floating-point result (7 / 2 results in 3.5). To get the same behavior in Python 2, you can use from __future__ import division or explicitly convert one of the numbers to a float.

3. **Unicode Strings:** Python 3 handles text data using Unicode by default, which provides broad support for characters from different languages. In Python 2, strings are treated as byte sequences (ASCII) unless you explicitly mark them with a u prefix (e.g., u"Hello").

4. **xrange vs. range:** In Python 2, the xrange function was used for generating sequences of numbers in a memory-efficient way. Python 3 replaced xrange with range, which now behaves like the old xrange. So, if you encounter xrange in older code, you can simply replace it with range in Python 3.

5. **Error Handling (Exceptions):** Python 3 uses the as keyword to assign the exception object in try-except blocks: except Exception as e:. In Python 2, you'd use a comma: except Exception, e:.

6. **Other Differences:**

   - The input() function in Python 2 behaves like eval(input()) in Python 3, leading to potential security risks.

   - Python 3 introduced many new features and improvements, such as f-strings, type hints, and better support for asynchronous programming.

Recommendation:

If you're starting a new project, always use Python 3. It's the future of the language and offers better features, performance, and community support. When working with existing Python 2 code, carefully consider the necessary changes to ensure a smooth transition to Python 3.

Key Takeaways:

- Python 3 is the recommended version for modern Python development.

- Be aware of the major differences when working with older Python 2 code.

- Prioritize writing code that is compatible with Python 3, as it is the future of the language.

Recipe 102: Migrating from Python 2 to Python 3

If you have existing Python 2 code that you need to update for Python 3 compatibility, here's a guide to help you through the transition:

1. Assess Your Code:

- **Identify Dependencies:** Check which libraries and modules your code relies on. Verify if they have Python 3-compatible versions available. If not, you might need to find alternatives or consider refactoring your code.

- **Compatibility Tools:** Use tools like caniusepython3 to see if your dependencies are Python 3-ready.

2. Use Automated Conversion Tools:

- **2to3:** This tool, included with Python 3, can automatically convert many common Python 2 patterns to Python 3 syntax. However, it might not catch all issues and might introduce some inefficiencies. Review the changes carefully.

- **python-modernize:** A tool built on top of 2to3 that aims to produce more modern and idiomatic Python 3 code.

- **futurize:** Another library that can help update your code to be compatible with both Python 2 and 3.

3. Manual Code Updates:

- **print Function:** Change print statements to function calls with parentheses: print("Hello").

- **Integer Division:** If you rely on integer division (7 / 2 resulting in 3), add from __future__ import division to your code or explicitly convert one of the numbers to a float.

- **Unicode Strings:** In Python 2, explicitly mark Unicode strings with u (e.g., u"Hello"). In Python 3, this is not needed as strings are Unicode by default.

- **xrange:** Replace xrange with range in Python 3.

- **Exceptions:** Update exception handling syntax to use as (e.g., except Exception as e:).

- **Library Changes:** Some modules and functions might have different names or behaviors in Python 3. Check the documentation for changes.

4. Testing:

- **Unit Tests:** If you have unit tests for your Python 2 code, run them against the updated Python 3 code to catch any issues early on.

- **Thorough Testing:** Test your code thoroughly with a variety of inputs and use cases to ensure it behaves as expected in Python 3.

5. Gradual Transition:

- If a complete conversion is not feasible, consider making incremental changes and testing regularly.

- You can use libraries like six to write code that works with both Python 2 and Python 3.

Example: Converting a print Statement:

```
# Python 2
print "Hello"
```

```
# Python 3
print("Hello")
```

Key Takeaways:

- Migrating to Python 3 is a valuable investment for the future.

- Automated tools can be helpful, but manual code updates and thorough testing are essential for a successful migration.

- Prioritize compatibility with Python 3, and take advantage of the modern features and improvements it offers.

Recipe 103: Common Pitfalls and How to Avoid Them

Even experienced Python programmers can fall into traps due to the language's flexibility and some subtle nuances. Let's explore some common pitfalls and how to steer clear of them:

1. **Mutable Default Arguments:**

   - **Pitfall:** Using mutable objects (like lists or dictionaries) as default arguments in functions can lead to unexpected behavior. The default value is shared across all calls to the function, and modifications in one call will affect subsequent calls.

   - **Solution:** Use None as the default and create the mutable object inside the function if the argument is not provided.

2. **Scope Confusion (Local vs. Global):**

   - **Pitfall:** Modifying a global variable from within a function requires explicitly declaring it as global. Otherwise, Python creates a new local variable with the same name.

   - **Solution:** Use global only when necessary. Consider passing values as arguments and returning results to avoid relying on global variables.

3. **Misunderstanding == vs. is:**

   - **Pitfall:** == checks for value equality, while is checks for object identity. For immutable objects (like numbers and strings), this might not matter, but for mutable objects, it's crucial.

- **Solution:** Use == for comparing values and is for comparing if two variables refer to the same object.

4. **Iterating While Modifying a List:**

- **Pitfall:** Modifying a list while iterating over it can lead to unexpected results (elements skipped or processed multiple times).

- **Solution:** Iterate over a copy of the list (for item in list_copy:) or use list comprehension for modifications.

5. **Misusing Expressions as Defaults:**

- **Pitfall:** Default values are evaluated only once when the function is defined. This can cause issues if you use mutable objects or expressions that rely on external state.

- **Solution:** Use None as a placeholder default and initialize the actual default value inside the function.

6. **Ignoring Unicode and Encodings:**

- **Pitfall:** Assuming all text is ASCII can lead to encoding errors when dealing with international characters.

- **Solution:** Use Unicode strings (str type in Python 3) by default and be mindful of encodings when reading/writing files or communicating over a network.

7. Incorrect Indentation:

- **Pitfall:** Python uses indentation to define code blocks. Incorrect indentation can lead to syntax errors or unintended behavior.

- **Solution:** Always use consistent indentation (spaces or tabs, but not both mixed). Many editors can automatically format your code correctly.

8. Unnecessary Global Variables:

- **Pitfall:** Overusing global variables can make your code harder to understand, test, and maintain.

- **Solution:** Limit the use of global variables. Pass data to functions through arguments and use return values for communication.

9. Circular Imports:

- **Pitfall:** When two (or more) modules import each other, it can create a circular dependency and lead to import errors.

- **Solution:** Carefully organize your modules, and import only what's necessary in each module. Consider refactoring your code if you encounter circular imports.

By being aware of these common pitfalls and applying the recommended solutions, you'll be well on your way to writing cleaner, more robust, and error-free Python code.

20. Conclusion:

Recipe 104: Recap of Key Python Concepts

Congratulations! You've journeyed through 100 Python recipes, each designed to empower you with practical skills and knowledge. Let's briefly revisit some of the essential concepts you've learned:

1. Fundamentals:

- **Variables and Data Types:** You've mastered integers, floats, strings, booleans, and more.

- **Operators:** Arithmetic, comparison, logical, and bitwise operations are now at your fingertips.

- **Control Flow:** if, elif, and else statements guide your program's decisions, while for and while loops handle repetitive tasks.

- **Functions:** You can create reusable blocks of code with parameters and return values, making your programs more organized and efficient.

- **Data Structures:** Lists, dictionaries, tuples, and sets offer powerful ways to store and manipulate collections of data.

2. Advanced Topics:

- **Object-Oriented Programming (OOP):** You've learned how to create classes and objects, harnessing the power of inheritance and polymorphism.

- **Modules and Packages:** Python's vast library of modules, including the standard library and external

packages
like requests, BeautifulSoup, and pandas, extend
Python's capabilities significantly.

- **File I/O:** You can read from and write to files, working
  with various formats like CSV and JSON.

- **Error Handling:** try-except blocks and custom
  exceptions help you create robust and reliable programs.

3. Additional Skills:

- **Web Scraping:** You can extract valuable data from
  websites to analyze and process.

- **GUI Development:** You can create graphical user
  interfaces using libraries like Tkinter.

- **Data Analysis:** Pandas and NumPy equip you to
  explore and analyze data effectively.

- **Machine Learning:** You've dipped your toes into the
  world of machine learning, gaining a foundation for
  building predictive models.

Beyond the Cookbook:

This ebook has been your guide, but the Python universe is vast
and ever-expanding. Continue your learning journey by:

- **Practicing Regularly:** Apply your knowledge to real-
  world projects and challenges.

- **Exploring the Documentation:** Dive deeper into the
  official Python documentation for comprehensive
  reference.

- **Joining the Community:** Engage with other Python
  enthusiasts through forums, websites, and social media.

- **Staying Curious:** Python is constantly evolving, so keep exploring new libraries, frameworks, and techniques.

Remember, the key to mastery is consistent practice and a hunger for knowledge. With dedication and the right resources, you'll continue to grow as a Python developer and create amazing things!

Recipe 105: Next Steps in Your Python Journey

Congratulations again on completing the Python Cookbook! You've now built a strong foundation in the language, covering everything from the basics to advanced topics like OOP, data analysis, and machine learning. But your Python journey doesn't end here—it's just the beginning!

Here are some exciting paths you can take to further enhance your skills and become a true Python pro:

1. Deep Dive into Specialized Areas:

- **Web Development:** Explore frameworks like Flask and Django to build full-fledged web applications, APIs, and dynamic websites.

- **Data Science:** Master libraries like Pandas, NumPy, and Matplotlib for data analysis, manipulation, and visualization.

- **Machine Learning:** Delve into scikit-learn, TensorFlow, or PyTorch to create predictive models, image recognition systems, or natural language processing applications.

- **Automation and Scripting:** Automate repetitive tasks at work or in your personal projects using Python's powerful scripting capabilities.

- **Game Development:** Create interactive games using libraries like Pygame or explore 3D game development with engines like Panda3D.

2. Explore the Python Ecosystem:

- **PyPI (Python Package Index):** Discover thousands of third-party libraries and packages that can supercharge your Python projects.

- **Virtual Environments:** Learn how to manage dependencies effectively using virtual environments (e.g., venv or conda).

- **IDEs and Code Editors:** Get comfortable with powerful Python-specific IDEs (Integrated Development Environments) like PyCharm or Visual Studio Code to streamline your development workflow.

3. Build Real-World Projects:

- **The best way to learn is by doing!** Tackle projects that interest you, whether it's building a personal website, creating a data analysis tool, or developing a simple game.

- **Contribute to Open Source:** Join the open-source community and collaborate with other developers to build and maintain Python projects. It's a great way to learn from others and make a meaningful contribution.

4. Stay Connected with the Community:

- **Join forums and online communities:** Participate in discussions, ask questions, and share your knowledge.

- **Attend conferences and meetups:** Connect with fellow Pythonistas in person to network and learn from experts.

5. Continuous Learning:

- **Read blogs and articles:** Stay updated on the latest Python trends, techniques, and best practices by reading articles and blog posts from reputable sources.

- **Take online courses:** Enroll in intermediate or advanced Python courses to expand your knowledge and skills.

- **Follow Python news:** Keep track of new releases and features in the Python ecosystem.

Remember:

Learning is a journey, not a destination. Embrace challenges, stay curious, and never stop exploring the endless possibilities Python has to offer!

About the Author

Ashish Prasad is a professional DevOps engineer with a deep-rooted passion for Python and its incredible ability to streamline workflows and automate the mundane. With many years of experience under their belt, they've harnessed Python's power to tackle a wide range of challenges, from optimizing complex software deployments to automating repetitive tasks that used to eat up valuable time.

Ashish's love for Python extends beyond the workplace. They're a firm believer in the language's accessibility and versatility, and they're dedicated to sharing their knowledge and enthusiasm with fellow developers.

This cookbook is a culmination of Ashish's real-world experience and their commitment to making Python approachable for everyone. Through carefully crafted recipes and engaging explanations, they hope to inspire others to discover the joy of coding and unleash Python's full potential in their own work and projects.

Connect with Ashish online:

- **LinkedIn:** www.linkedin.com/in/ashishprasad133